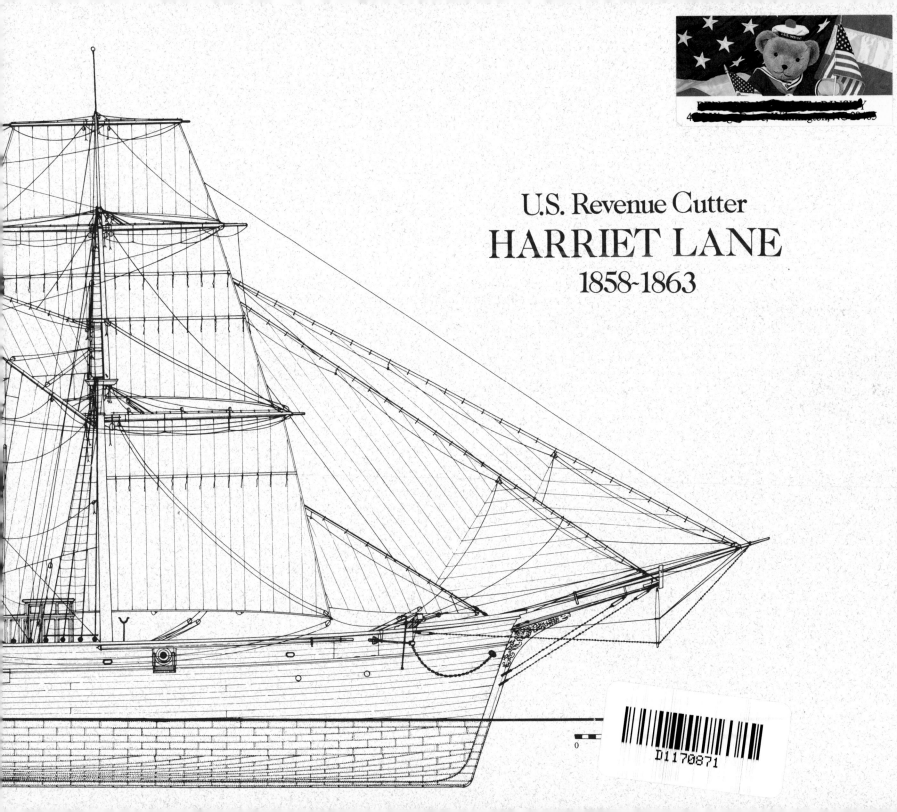

U.S. Revenue Cutter

HARRIET LANE

1858~1863

THEY THAT GO DOWN TO THE SEA

Foreword by Alex Haley

Text by PAC Paul A. Powers

A Bicentennial Pictorial History
of the United States Coast Guard

United States Coast Guard Chief Petty Officers Association

Published by United States Coast Guard
Chief Petty Officers Association
5520-G Hempstead Way
Springfield, Virginia 22151

Printed by Taylor Publishing Company
Dallas, Texas

Book design by Jan Jones Pulley

Library of Congress Catalog Card Number: 90-61231
ISBN 0-9626717-0-3 (Standard Edition)
ISBN 0-9626717-1-1 (Collector's Edition)

They that go down to the sea in ships,
 they that do business in great waters:
These see the works of the Lord,
 and his wonders in the deep.

Psalm 107

Contents

The First Century

The Second Century

Foreword

It is appropriate that the launching of this book should occur in 1990, the 200th anniversary of the U.S. Coast Guard's founding. I am among the many Coast Guard retirees who are likely to comprise the book's major market. Our careers have left us with a nostalgia for events which we each experienced in the oldest continuous sea-going service in the United States.

As a writer, whose first writing efforts were made at night, usually at sea, on the mess tables of various Coast Guard cutters, I can remember stories I loved to write of the now legendary Coast Guard lighthouses, and of their gripping dramas. For instance, I remember writing about one middle-aged light-keeper couple who awakened to see an ice-laden four-master impaled on a reef during the night, and the only survivor washed ashore, lashed tightly within blankets in a basket — an unidentified infant girl, whom the state of Massachusetts let the light-keeper couple adopt.

I used to love to sit around the real old-timer wearers of the shield, and hear their gripping personal tales of hair-raising Coast Guard responses and feats of rescue where ships of all sorts had wrecked, foundered, caught fire, sprung serious leaks, or otherwise courted tragedy. Especially valiant in this area were the truly fearless personnel of the now-historic surf stations, whose rescue surfboats achieved life-saving miracles that made the surfmen, such as those at the famed Pea Island Station, literally legends in their own time.

Even the classic lightships, those floating beacons of the sea, were vulnerable to being sideswiped by large passing ships. There was the tragedy which befell the TITANIC, which led to the U.S. Coast Guard's perennial International Ice Patrol, conducted both by air and sea, so that no big berg lurks in any sea lanes unannounced. There have been many thousands of search and rescue missions, involving everything from small craft to huge cargo ships and passenger liners. No one can count how many sea miles have been sailed by Coast Guard cutters on their grids on boring ocean patrol, away out there, in readiness for whatever might occur — as when a major airliner laden with passengers had to ditch into the Atlantic, on Ocean Station Charlie, and the patrolling Coast Guard Cutter BIBB, revved up to flank speed, was quickly there, saving air passengers. The world sighed in relief, and everybody in the Coast Guard walked a little taller.

I could go on and on, but that would be to ignore the present-day achievements of the Coast Guard, about which I am far less able to speak authoritatively. For me, nothing more graphically illustrates some of the new, modern Coast Guard's frequent bewilderments for us old-timers than how the names of ratings have been changed. Recently I was in Milwaukee, to speak at an anniversary ball, when I mentioned that I'd been a Coast Guard cook. I was told that a cook nowadays is termed a "subsistence specialist," for Pete's sake! I couldn't help remarking how that sounds to me like someone trying to cook with test tubes instead of pots and pans, as we used to.

Make no mistake, the modern U.S. Coast Guard is awesome. I'm very much perplexed about how I, long retired, can do justice to describing, even identifying, the vast range of Coast Guard functions performed today. I'll simply say that we'd have to live in some other country not to be aware of the Coast Guard's roles in drug interdiction, in countering ocean oil spills, in marine ecology, and in ongoing search and rescue, not to mention scores of other activities, which require the maximum capacities of the men and women of today's Coast Guard, whom all of us older-timers proudly salute with. . .

Semper Paratus!

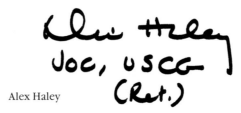

Alex Haley

Preface

The concept of this book was originally discussed in late October 1988, during a telephone conversation between the National Executive Secretary of the USCG Chief Petty Officers Association (CPOA), and a representative of Taylor Publishing Company. With the upcoming 200th anniversary of the U.S. Coast Guard, it appeared to be the ideal time to publish a bicentennial history of the U.S. Coast Guard. It was to be primarily a photographic history, but was also to contain a good deal of textual material. With publication of this book, we believe the objectives have been accomplished.

We started with the early Revenue Cutters from 1790, and then progressed through many of the "wars," insurrections and activities throughout the entire 200-year development of the U.S. Coast Guard. You will see articles and photographs concerning the Lighthouse Service, Life-Saving Service, World War I, Ice Patrols, Prohibition, WWII, Korea, Vietnam and Law Enforcement. Also the introduction of the SPARS, reserves, auxiliarists and the evolution of cutters, and aircraft.

A great number of individuals contributed materially to the success of this project. Some of those include Dr. Robert Scheina and Dr. Robert Browning, for advice and direct assistance. Credit for the text goes to CPOA member, PAC Paul A. Powers.

Realistically, however, we must give thanks to those CPOA members who dug through their individual memoirs to come up with ideas and photographs. They were numerous and greatly appreciated. Also, without those individuals with enough faith in the project to obligate funds for actual purchase of the book in advance of publication, this book could never have been published.

Special thanks to Susan McDonald, representative of Taylor Publishing Company.

C. R. "Dick" Castor
National Executive Secretary
USCG Chief Petty Officers Association

Acknowledgments

The information in this book has come from a wide variety of sources, both published and unpublished. The unpublished collection called *Some Unusual Incidents in Coast Guard History* contained many of the early anecdotes. Dr. Johnson's book *Guardians of the Sea* was very important for the latter part of the book. Johnson's very fine work is about the only history of the modern Coast Guard written by someone not connected with the Service. The Coast Guard bicentennial series, written in larger part by Dr. & Senior Chief Dennis L. Noble, USCG, ret., was also used extensively.

The writings of Dr. Bob Browning, Master Chief Dave Cipra, USCG (ret), Florence Kern and Irving H. King were critical for certain sections. My father, James J. Powers, proofread the text. Finally, I would like to thank Dr. Robert Scheina, who allowed me to use both his published and unpublished work and critiqued the manuscript.

Paul A. Powers

THE
FIRST
CENTURY

Early Revenue Cutter Sailors

The history of the Coast Guard closely parallels the development of the United States. Throughout its 200 years, the service has changed along with America's maritime needs. And as a result of this, many crucial moments in the story of America are also crucial moments in Coast Guard history.

The service was created to stop a very popular and profitable American pastime — smuggling.

After the Revolutionary War, the United States was in desperate need of money. Almost all of the nation's revenues came from taxes on imported goods. Unfortunately, many Americans developed a taste for smuggling during British rule and refused to stop after independence.

The Secretary of the Treasury, Alexander Hamilton, asked President George Washington for revenue cutters to stop the smugglers at sea. On August 4th, 1790 Congress started what we call today the U.S. Coast Guard when it authorized the construction of ten revenue cutters.

Many records relating to those early cutters have been destroyed, but the first one commissioned was probably the MASSACHU-SETTS, which was built in Newburyport, Mass. Eight of the 10 were topsail schooners the other two were sloops. The schooners were fast, sturdy boats with the Chesapeake Bay rigging favored by many U.S. coastal vessels. The cutters were all smaller than today's patrol boats. They averaged between 40 and 60 feet.

The first cutters were built under the eyes of the captains who would eventually command them, but Hamilton personally kept track of construction costs, and he was quick to write stern warnings to the captains if he thought the bills were exceeding appropriations.

Before the first cutter was launched, the Revenue Cutter Service's history of battling

Alexander Hamilton, ▶ the first Secretary of the United States Treasury, requested the purchase of revenue cutters to stop smuggling at sea.

3

Hopley Yeaton ▶ (pointing) was the first officer of the Revenue Cutter Service, but more important, he was the first Maritime Officer appointed under the Constitution.

◄ The MASSACHUSETTS was one of the first ten cutters appropriated in 1790. She was home-ported at Newburyport.

smugglers began thanks to a black woman named Marie Lee — better known as Black Marie.

Marie was a teamster and charged with delivering the cutter SCAMMEL's swivel guns from the foundries in Philadelphia to Portsmouth, New Hampshire where the cutter was

being built. Hopley Yeaton, the first Coast Guard captain, was in charge of supervising the construction of the SCAMMEL.

Smugglers from the lower Delaware Bay heard of the delivery and decided they wanted the guns for themselves. Six smugglers ambushed Marie on the road between

Philadelphia and New York. This was a big mistake. Marie tore into the smugglers and beat them all senseless. She then got back on the wagon and continued her journey.

Marie later opened a sailors' boarding house in Boston and continued to battle the lawless elements of society. Whenever a particularly troublesome person had to be taken to jail, the authorities called upon "Black Marie" for assistance.

The fight against smugglers began in earnest once the revenue cutter fleet was commissioned. The new cutters were stationed from New Hampshire to Georgia. Little is known about the first Revenue Cutter sailors. The majority of the captains were former members of the disbanded Continental Navy or the numerous state navies which had existed during the American Revolution.

Many of the crewmen were undoubtedly from the same sea services. They were also from the areas where the cutters were stationed. There were no enlistment hitches at the time and a new crew was hired at the dock for each season. A season generally lasted from six to nine months depending on the weather.

The job of the first Revenue Cutter sailors would be very familiar to many of today's Coast Guardsmen. They went out on law enforcement patrols. They boarded merchant ships at sea and checked the cargo manifest. If they found unlisted items on board, they assumed the captain was smuggling, and escorted the vessel to the nearest customs house.

Life at sea during those days was not pleasant for Revenue Cuttermen or for any sailors. There were no safety lines in the rigging, and men could easily fall to their deaths. The service spent nine cents a day for each crewman's rations, and sailors ate a monotonous diet of beef or pork and bread.

Fire was not permitted below deck because of the very great risk of an accident. A ship was a floating tinderbox of wood covered with pitch and tar. The only fire permitted on board was in the galley for cooking and even that was closely watched. So the men slept in cold, dark, damp corners of the cutter. Older sailors were almost always crippled with rheumatism and arthritis. Rats, fleas, ticks, lice and bed bugs were the sailors' constant companions.

However, it should be remembered that life on land during those days was not much better, and in spite of all the hardships, the early Revenue Cuttermen must have done their jobs well. Congress was certainly impressed with their work. A few years after Hamilton's fleet set sail, Congress authorized the construction of larger more heavily armed revenue cutters. They were built just in time to fight in the Quasi-War with France.

The cutter PICKERING ► served in the Quasi-War with France between 1798 and 1800, during which time she made 10 captures. She also won a nine-hour engagement with the large French privateer EGYPTE CONQUISE.

Quasi-War with France and the War of 1812

The Quasi-War with France was not one of America's big wars, but it was the first war under the Constitution, and the Revenue Cutter Service played a vital role.

The war was fought in 1798-1800 in order to secure free trade. At the time the English and the French were in the middle of one of their many wars, and the French objected to America's continued trade with Great Britain.

The French sent several warships as well as numerous privateers from their Caribbean islands to capture American merchant ships. Privateers were private citizens commissioned by a country to capture enemy vessels. For obvious reasons, these privateers preyed on the enemy's merchant ships and ran from its warships. Many nations, including the United States, have used privateers.

Revenue cutters and the newly created United States Navy (the Continental Navy had been disbanded in 1785) went after the privateers and French naval vessels. The Revenue Cutter Service made up one-third of America's naval force. The Service captured 23 enemy vessels, took three foreign merchant ships and recaptured 10 American vessels that had been taken by the French.

French military problems in Europe and U.S. naval successes led to a negotiated settlement to end this conflict in 1800. The peace did not last very long. Twelve years later the United States was fighting England in the War of 1812.

Once again the English and the French were in the middle of one of their many wars. England desperately needed trained seaman and took them from American merchant ships by force if necessary. Some of these impressed sailors were Englishmen who had deserted from the British Navy, but some of them were American citizens. The United States went to war to stop this practice and secure the nation's trade rights. Both the English fleet and British privateers fought the Americans.

The revenue cutters were far too small to fight the British warships which crossed the Atlantic, so they pursued the privateers. In one well-known engagement the revenue cutter VIGILANT captured the notorious British privateer DART. The DART had captured 20 to 30 American merchant vessels in Long Island Sound before the VIGILANT ended its career.

There were many other successes, but two revenue cutter defeats are worth noting, because they tell a lot about the spirit of the men.

In one engagement, the revenue cutter EAGLE was being chased by the English 18-gun DISPATCH and two other vessels near Long Island, New York. The cutter was intentionally grounded, the guns were removed and dragged to a high bluff where the men

**The VIGILANT sails ►
out to do battle with the
privateer DART, which
had been terrorizing
American commerce,
4 October 1813.**

up all their ammunition, they picked up British shot and fired them back. The EAGLE was refloated by the Americans after the battle and was captured by the British.

In another incident, the revenue cutter SURVEYOR was attacked by the much larger British frigate NARCISSUS. The Revenue Cuttermen fought a brief and desperate battle against the British boarding party. Five of the SURVEYOR's crewmen were wounded, but they killed three and wounded seven of the enemy before being captured. The British captain was so impressed with the fighting spirit of the SURVEYOR's men that he returned the captain's sword the next day with the following note.

"Your gallant and desperate attempt to defend your vessel against more than double your number on the night of the 12th excited such admiration on the part of your opponents as I have seldom witnessed and induced me to return the sword you had so nobly used, in testimony of mine. . ."

A peace treaty between the United States and Great Britain was signed on Dec. 24, 1814 at Ghent, Belgium. The United States and Great Britain both made concessions.

1813 to 1860

Between the War of 1812 and the Civil War, Revenue Cuttermen fought in two wars, enforced federal laws and continued to go after pirates, privateers and slavers.

Many of the pirates and privateers came from South America. They generally preyed on ships around Florida and in the Gulf of Mexico but they occasionally attacked vessels as far north as the Chesapeake Bay in Maryland. The cutters ALABAMA and LOUISIANA were particularly effective in ridding the Gulf of Mexico of pirates. The vessels were both 57 feet in length, 17 feet in beam and had a shallow six-foot draft. In 1819, they were stationed in New Orleans.

On their maiden voyage south, the LOUISIANA and the ALABAMA battled and captured the pirate ship BRAVO, north of the Tortugas as it was making off with two prizes. After boarding one of the prizes the ALABAMA reported:

"She was laden with flour and when she was taken had on a number of passengers, both ladies and gentlemen, who were treated by the pirates in the most shameful manner. They were robbed of everything, even to the clothes on their backs, and when the ladies begged for something to cover them, the pirates drew their swords on them, using the most brutal language."

The BRAVO's captain was Jean Defarges, who was the lieutenant of the notorious pirate Jean Lafitte. Defarges was later hanged from the yardarm of the LOUISIANA.

The Revenue Cutter ▶ MCLEAN, one of several sent to Charleston to assure collection of federal taxes.

On another fruitful 20-day cruise, the LOUISIANA captured four pirate ships. The cutters also attacked pirates on land. Together, they destroyed Patterson's Town, the pirate's den on Breton Island. They torched the houses and the woods and the fires "consumed everything that was standing." This practically put an end to piracy in the Gulf.

Revenue Cutter sailors fought the slaver trade from 1794 to 1861. During that time they freed 487 slaves, but many more slaves died at sea. Revenue cutters often chased slave boats only to find no slaves on board when the ship was taken. But they knew slaves had been on board a few hours earlier because of the stench in the unsanitary holds.

Revenue Cuttermen also found themselves in the middle of the growing hostility between the North and the South, which simmered for many years before the outbreak of the Civil War. A constant sore point between the Northerners and the Southerners was the division of power between the states and the federal government. The Southerners favored strong states' rights, the Northerners favored a strong federal government.

In 1832 in Charleston, S.C. the Revenue Cutter Service enforced federal authority by collecting a protective tariff on sugar. The southern states were opposed to the tariff and no longer recognized the federal government's right to collect it. The revenue cutters assisted the customs collectors for four months before a law was passed which gradually lowered duties over a period of years.

Four years later, the Seminole Indian Wars resumed in Florida after a forced Indian resettlement. It turned into a seven-year battle of treacherous swamp warfare. The Army, the Navy and the Revenue Cutter Service chased a seemingly invisible enemy across the swamps. Over the years, Revenue Cutter sailors landed men on the shore, repulsed attacks and captured Indian supplies. The war ended when there were only 120 Seminoles capable of bearing arms.

Three years after the Seminole Indian War, the United States annexed Texas and went to war with Mexico. The war was started after a Mexican cavalry unit attacked a cavalry unit from the United States north of the Rio Grande, territory claimed by both nations. Revenue cutters set sail for Texas in 1846 to help the American Army. They delivered supplies, worked blockade duty, convoyed troops and helped enforce American customs laws.

There were several other interesting developments in this period which affected the Revenue Cutter Service.

On Dec. 16, 1831, the GALLATIN received orders to begin lifesaving patrols. This was the first time that revenue cutters were ordered to sea solely to assist vessels, although the tradition of aiding those in distress had been in effect since 1790.

In 1844, the Service purchased its first four iron steam cutters. Unfortunately, they chose a terrible design. The cutters were a total disaster. They were expensive, slow as molasses, constantly broke down and burned an unbelievable amount of coal. The Revenue Cutter Service "rewarded" the officer who suggested the design by putting him in command of one the cutters.

The Service reverted to sail in 1848, but these first steam ships created the need for a new type of Revenue Cutterman — the engineer. The first six engineers were appointed on March 3, 1845. The Service also allowed the enlistment of "landsmen" with mechanical ability — until this time only experienced seamen were recruited.

Civil War 1861-1865

The Civil War tore apart the Revenue Cutter Service, along with the rest of the nation. At the outbreak of the war, five cutters and a large number of lighthouse tenders were either captured or voluntarily turned over to the Confederacy, while many officers and men left the service to follow the southern cause.

There were only 28 effective cutters at the outbreak of the war, two of them were in the Pacific and five were on the Great Lakes. Over time, the Service was built up to 48 vessels by bringing back decommissioned cutters, taking ships from the coastal survey, converting merchantmen into cutters, using boats donated by private citizens and by building six new screw-steamers.

Revenue Cuttermen not only saw action from the very beginning of the war, they opened the Civil War's naval conflict. The side-wheeler cutter HARRIET LANE fired the first naval shot at the steamship NASHVILLE as it entered Charleston Harbor during the Confederate bombardment of Fort Sumter. The NASHVILLE was allowed to pass once it raised the American flag. The Confederate troops captured the fort two days later while the HARRIET LANE and the Navy relief squadron stood outside the harbor unable to help.

During the war, revenue cutters worked closely with the Army and Navy and performed a wide variety of tasks. They searched for Confederate privateers, enforced customs laws, landed troops, and blockaded harbors. One cutter, the steamer MIAMI, served as President Lincoln's personal transport.

In one strange incident in May 1862, the president and the Secretaries of War and Treasury were on board the MIAMI trying to decide if they should attack Norfolk. The MIAMI took the president and his party to the proposed landing site. Lincoln reconnoitered the area and saw it was lightly defended. He ordered an attack the next day. The Union Army landed, fought off light resistance and entered the deserted city of Norfolk.

The surrender by General Robert E. Lee in April 1865 did not end the involvement of the Revenue Cutter Service in the South. After the war, they helped re-establish customs houses and rebuild southern commerce.

1898 — Spanish-American War

The Spanish-American War was America's last 19th century war. It was sparked by the sinking of the USS MAINE in Havana Harbor. Its conclusion ended Spain's involvement in Cuba and the Philippines and helped establish America as a world power.

Thirteen revenue cutters worked with the Navy during the war. Eight of them were in the North Atlantic squadron, one was in the Asiatic Squadron and four were on the Pacific Coast of the United States. Seven other cutters worked with the Army patrolling mine fields in harbors from Boston to New Orleans.

One of the most dramatic incidents of that war was a rescue of the naval torpedo boat WINSLOW by the revenue cutter HUDSON at Cardenas Bay, Cuba. The WINSLOW was disabled by shore batteries. The ship's captain was wounded, one officer and several crewmen were killed. While under fire from shore, the cutter HUDSON, which was a tug boat, returned fire with its six-pounder gun and rushed to the aid of the damaged naval vessel. Fierce fire was directed against the HUDSON and the WINSLOW. Shells were dropping all around the tug and one actually hit the cutter but did not explode. The HUDSON managed to get a line on the torpedo boat and towed it to safety.

◄ **The HARRIET LANE fires the first maritime shot of the Civil War as she challenges the steamer NASHVILLE, which attempted to enter port without identifying herself.**

Cutter BEAR in Alaska

With the end of the Spanish-American War, the 19th century drew to an end. However, the history of the Revenue Cutter Service during this period would be incomplete without mention of the cutter BEAR and its impact on Alaskan history.

The Coast Guard has had a considerable impact on Alaskan history for more than 100 years. A good bit of that history can be found in the log books of the BEAR. The BEAR was a 200-foot steam barkentine which went to Alaska in 1886 and served more than 40 years in the north. During that time, its duties and accomplishments matched the monumental scale of the territory it protected.

The BEAR did not just enforce federal laws in Alaska; it was the law. The BEAR was the most important federal presence in the territories for many years. This period included the wild, lawless Gold Rush days.

The BEAR protected seal herds; the BEAR guarded salmon fisheries; the BEAR even took the first reindeer to Alaska. The reindeer were carried by the BEAR from Siberia to

◄ **During the Spanish-American War, cutters served with U. S. naval forces in the Pacific and the Caribbean. The cutter HUDSON rescues the damaged USS WINSLOW from Spanish land batteries off Cardenas Bay, Cuba.**

supplement the food supply of the Native Americans.

The BEAR's most famous rescue involved

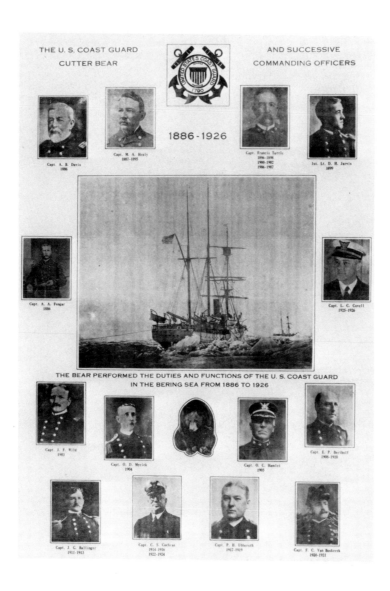

THE U. S. COAST GUARD CUTTER BEAR AND SUCCESSIVE COMMANDING OFFICERS

1886 - 1926

THE BEAR PERFORMED THE DUTIES AND FUNCTIONS OF THE U. S. COAST GUARD IN THE BERING SEA FROM 1886 TO 1926

Depicted here is the U. S. Coast Guard Cutter BEAR locked in ice on August 7, 1898, after picking up 97 shipwrecked whalers east of Point Barrow, Alaska *(following page).*

five ships and a horrendous overland journey. It occurred in the winter of 1897. A whaling fleet was trapped east of Point Barrow along the North Slope, and the BEAR was sent to the rescue. The cutter went as far north as it could and then a shore party drove a herd of 400 reindeer 1,600 miles to the trapped men. The whalers and the Revenue Cuttermen lived off the reindeer until the BEAR reached them in the spring. The Eskimos regarded the BEAR as having a charmed life and considered its captain to be a direct representative of the King of Kings.

The BEAR served with the Navy in Greenland during World War II and was later sold. Its long history came to an end on March 17, 1963 when it sank during a storm off Massachusetts while being towed from Newfoundland to Philadelphia.

These brief highlights of the Revenue Cutter Service's first 100 years are only a part of the Coast Guard story. The U.S. Lighthouse Service, the U.S. Life-Saving Service, the Steamboat Inspection Service and the Bureau of Navigation are also branches of the Coast Guard. These organizations have their own fascinating histories.

Officers on board the U. S. Revenue Cutter BEAR when she made the Relief Expedition for the stranded whalers at Point Barrow, Alaska, 1897-1898. L to R - Seated 1st row: 3rd Lieut. Bernard H. Camden; 1st Asst. Engineer Herbert W. Spear. 2nd row: 2nd Lieut. John G. Berry; Capt. Francis Tuttle-Commanding; 2nd Lieut. Claude S. Cochran; 1st Lieut. James H. Brown. Back row: 2nd Asst. Engineer John I. Bryan; 1st Asst. Engineer Horatio N. Wood. Last names of these officers were identified by RADM Thomas M. Molloy, on April 10, 1944 *(preceding page)*.

◄ Crew aloft unfurling the sails on the U. S. Revenue Cutter BEAR, circa 1890s.

A grave site of a ► Revenue Cutter BEAR sailor in a desolate and nearly forgotten cemetery in the city of Unalaska, an area routinely patrolled by the famous BEAR.

The Lighthouse Service

At their peak in the early 20th century, there were about 1,200 manned lighthouses in the United States. Today, they are virtually all automated and nearly all the keepers are gone. People still live in some of them, but they do not take care of the lights. The new tenants run inns, youth hostels or local museums. A few Coast Guardsmen from nearby units also live in lighthouses.

Some of America's lighthouses are national treasures dating back to colonial times. The first lighthouse built in the North American colonies was Boston Light, built on Little Brewster Island in 1716. It was destroyed by the British in 1776 and the present structure was erected in 1783. The oldest standing tower in America was built in 1764 at Sandy Hook, N.J.

Many lightstations are engineering marvels. St. George Reef Light off Northern California, Minots Ledge off Massachusetts, and Tillamook Rock off Oregon were built in terrible seas on wave-swept rocks. Others are elegant structures reflecting the very best in the architecture of the time.

These old buildings seem to occupy a special place in the hearts of many Americans. Tourists see these beautiful structures on prime pieces of ocean front real estate and instantly want to move in.

In the old days, lighthouse duty could be quite desirable at the right station. For the

Portland Head ▶ **Lighthouse was the first to be completed following the adoption of the Constitution.**

◀ **Little Brewster Island is the site of this nation's first lighthouse. The current tower, known as Boston Harbor Lighthouse, is the third to be erected on this island.**

The following is ▶ **quoted from "Lighthouses and Lightships" by George R. Putnam: "In 1719 the keeper petitioned the General Court 'that a great Gun be placed on Said Island to answer Ships in a Fog.' The Court voted the gun, and it was probably the earliest fog signal established in the Country. Though long since out of service for this purpose, this cannon is still at Boston Light Station; it bears the date 1700."**

◄ **Keeper of the Boston Light, Ralph Norwood, BM2/c, U. S. Coast Guard, is seen here in September, 1941, working on the burner of the light.**

Construction of the ► **St. George Reef Lighthouse. This photo was found by the Keeper in station files in 1938. The station was built in 1892 out of 1,339 dressed granite blocks from Mad River at a cost of $712,000. In addition to being one of the most expensive light stations built during that period, eight years were required for completion of the station.**

Seen here in 1931, ► **the loading of supplies with a 90-foot steel boom at the St. George Reef Lighthouse.**

Saint George Reef Light is located 134 feet above sea level at a point approximately 10 miles west of Crescent City Harbor and is a fully automated 250,000 candlepower light, fog signal, and radio beacon *(following page).*

most part, the work was not very difficult. Before the days of electricity the lights were lit with a variety of oils, including whale oil, vegetable oils, lard and kerosine. During the night the keepers would check the lights hourly to make sure everything was in working order. The lights, which revolved, were turned by a clock-like mechanism attached to weights which hung down the tower. The keepers had to wind the machinery every four hours. In the morning they would polish the brass and trim the wicks. The wicks were trimmed regularly to insure a bright flame and because of this job, the keepers were called "wickies."

The brass had to be kept spotless because

9 Dist.

Minots Ledge, Mass.
At sunrise, Sunday morning, 7/11/58.
"Laying the lowest stone in the
structure"

Saint George Reef Lighthouse off the northern California coast is one of a few wave-swept towers built in this country *(preceding page).*

◄ **Minots Ledge at Cohasset, Massachusetts, was completed (second lighthouse) in 1860 with much of its foundation being underwater. The first 40 feet of the tower is solid stone. This tower is 97 feet tall and has been topped by a wave at least twice.**

◄ **Minots Ledge on July 11, 1858, at the laying of the lowest stone.**

Tillamook Rock, another wave-swept light, is built off the Oregon coast. These photos were taken by the 13th District office in October, 1971 *(following pages).*

the lighthouse inspectors, who were often terrors, paid particular attention to the brass. However, they were quick to write up a keeper for just about anything. One keeper was cited for using up his supply of pencils too quickly.

The brass, however, was the big problem. There was even a song written about polishing brass: it was called "On Brasswork."

> *Oh, what is the bane of a lightkeeper's life,*
> *That causes him worry and struggle and strife,*
> *That makes him use cuss words and beat up his wife,*
> *It's brasswork.*
> *The lamp in the tower, reflector and shade,*
> *The tools and accessories pass in parade,*
> *As a matter of fact the whole outfit is made,*
> *Of brasswork.*
> *I dig, scrub and polish, and work with a might.*
> *And just when I get it all shining and bright,*
> *In comes the fog like a thief in the night.*
> *Good-bye brasswork.*
> *And when I have polished until I am cold,*
> *And I'm taken aloft to the heavenly fold,*
> *Will my harp and my crown be made of pure gold?*
> *No Brasswork!*

At the more isolated stations lighthouse duty could be lonely, monotonous work. Many people disliked the lack of human contact but others thrived on it. One turn-of-the-century keeper at isolated Tillamook Rock

couldn't get enough of the place. As a reward for excellent service he was sent to San Francisco to take care of the Service's exhibit in the Panama-Pacific Exposition. After a week in the big city, he asked to be sent back to the rock. And after 25-years' duty on Tillamook, he retired and asked if he could live there for the rest of his life.

The lighthouse was often a family affair. Many wives were assistant keepers and several became keepers after their husbands died. Some of the Lighthouse Service's most interesting stories revolve around women and families.

During the War of 1812, Rebecca and Abigail Bates, the daughters of Keeper Simeon Bates at Scituate Light, were credited with stopping a British invasion. The incident occurred in September 1814. The British man-of-war LA HOGUE had anchored near the lighthouse. The two girls and their younger brother were the only people at the station. The girls sent their brother to warn the local villagers, and then they watched as five of the warship's longboats made their way towards the shore.

Rebecca grabbed a drum and gave her sister Abigail a fife. They began to play martial music and tricked the British into thinking a large armed force was on shore. The British landing party returned to its ship and the girls collapsed in exhaustion.

The most famous keeper of them all was a Rhode Island woman named Idawalla Zorada Lewis. Ida came to the Lime Rock lighthouse in Newport Harbor as a young girl and

became the keeper after her father died. During her early years at the lighthouse, Ida rowed her younger brother and sister back and forth to the mainland so that they could go to school. As a result of this chore, she developed outstanding boat-handling skills which were put to the test many times over.

Ida became the Lighthouse Service's most famous lifesaver. She performed her first rescue at the age of 16, when she saved four young men who were clinging to a capsized sailboat. During her more than 40 years at the lighthouse, she rescued at least 19 people. Her lifesaving feats made her a national celebrity. Young girls wore their hair "Ida Lewis style" and boys wore Ida Lewis scarfs. She was writ-

ten up in Harper's and Leslie's magazines and she even received a visit from President Ulysses S. Grant.

Ida's last rescue was at the age of 64. A friend capsized her boat on the way to Lime Rock light. Ida launched her heavy wooden boat and pulled the woman out of the water. Ida died on October 24, 1911. On that night, the bells of all the vessels anchored in Newport Harbor tolled in her honor. The Lighthouse Board renamed Lime Rock light the Ida Lewis lighthouse, the only time such an honor was given.

Ida Lewis was just one of many heroes of the Lighthouse Service. Scores of dramatic rescues were carried out by keepers.

Seen here are the ►
Keeper and his family of the Sentinel Island Light Station. This was one of the first lighthouses built in southeast Alaska. It was erected in 1902.

◄
(left) **Fourth-order fixed lens used at Drum Point, Maryland.**

(center) **First-order clam shell classical lens at Rock of Ages Lighthouse, Michigan.**

(right) **Third-order lens at Shore Village Museum in Rockland, Maine.**

Ida Lewis ▶

◀ *(Left)* **In 1925 following the death of her husband, President Calvin Coolidge named Fannie Salter as lighthouse keeper among the nation's 7,500 keepers. She was keeper of the lighthouse at Turkey Point, at the head of the Chesapeake Bay for 22 years. She retired in 1947. She is shown in a 1954 photo, polishing the lens in the lighthouse at Turkey Point. (Mobile Press Register UPI Telephoto)**

◀ *(Right)* **Harriet A. Colfax, light keeper, at Indiana's Michigan City Lighthouse for more than 40 years.**

◀ **Lime Rock Lighthouse in Newport Harbor, Rhode Island, was renamed the Ida Lewis Lighthouse to honor the famous female keeper who worked at this light for over 50 years.**

HARPER'S WEEKLY.
A JOURNAL OF CIVILIZATION.

VOL. XIII.—No. 657.]　　NEW YORK, SATURDAY, JULY 31, 1869.　　[SINGLE COPIES, TEN CENTS. $4.00 PER YEAR IN ADVANCE.

Entered according to Act of Congress, in the Year 1869, by Harper & Brothers, in the Clerk's Office of the District Court of the United States, for the Southern District of New York.

MISS IDA LEWIS, THE HEROINE OF NEWPORT.—Phot. by Manchester Brothers, Providence, R. I.—[See Page 484.]

Lightships

Today's automated lighthouses may no longer have the human touch, but they are still operating. Another navigational aid, the lightship, can be found only in maritime museums. Lightships were floating lighthouses positioned in locations where it was impossible to build lightstations.

The first light vessel, the Craney Island Lightship Station, was established in Hampton Roads at the entrance to Elizabeth River in 1820. Hundreds of these vessels have been stationed on exposed, open ocean locations since then. These little lightships were at times run down by much larger vessels. The Ambrose Channel station was the most dangerous. During its 56-year existence, the lightship was hit four times.

One of the most tragic disasters occurred on May 16, 1934, when the OLYMPIC, the sister ship of the TITANIC, plowed into the NANTUCKET SHOALS lightship. The liner had been steering on the lightship's radio beacon when it ran into dense fog. It hit the lightship at only two or three knots, but the tremendous weight of the 45,000-ton liner crushed the small vessel. The lightship sank instantly with the loss of seven men.

Technology finally caught up with lightships. They have all been replaced by either large buoys or platforms with supports driven into the seabed.

◄ Photo of the Nantucket Lightship was taken 200 feet off the starboard beam. This lightship station was established in 1892.

◄ Scotland Lightship marks the southerly approach to the entrance to New York Harbor. Its name "Scotland" is taken from a vessel wrecked here more than half a century ago.

An aerial view of ▶
the emergency beacon
and main beacon lights
of the Ambrose
Lightship.

▼ Its 13,000 candle-
power light glowing
from sundown to sun-
rise, its red hull with
white lettering sharply
visible in daytime, San
Francisco Lightship
stood a 24-hour vigi-
lance at the entrance to
the Golden Gate and
San Francisco guiding
marine traffic. Shining
from the foremast of
the two-masted light-
ship 65 feet above
water, the light could be
seen from a distance of
14 miles from the sea
on clear days. The ship
lay at anchor in 108
feet of water.

U.S. Life-Saving Service

The United States has a long history of saving lives at sea. In 1785, a volunteer lifesaving organization called the Massachusetts Humane Society was formed to help people on vessels in distress. They built the first lifesaving station in the United States in 1807 at Cohasset, Massachusetts. The Chinese and the British were the only people that built lifesaving stations before the Americans. The Chinese built the first known stations on the Min River and its tributaries in 1737. The British built their first station in 1786 at Bamborough Castle, England.

The U.S. federal government began funding lifeboat stations in 1847, when money for boathouses and equipment on Cape Cod was given to the Massachusetts Humane Society. The first stations built with federal funds were constructed the following year on the New Jersey coast between Sandy Hook and Little Egg Harbor. Eight boathouses, each about 16 by 28 feet, were built under the direction of the Revenue Marine, one of the many former names for the Coast Guard. They were little more than scantily equipped shacks and Congress did not authorize money for keepers.

The keys to the stations were simply left with the nearest responsible person, who was also given a printed card with instructions on how to use the equipment. Many of the unpaid volunteers did a good job, but overall the system did not work very well. The unguarded boats and stations fell into disrepair.

A tragedy off Long Beach, N.Y. finally galvanized the public, and Congress approved money for keepers. The accident occurred on April 16, 1854. The immigrant ship POWHATAN smashed into the shore during a terrible gale, and 311 men, women and children died in the surf while those on shore could do little more than pull dead bodies out of the water.

◄ Sumner Increase Kimball held the position of General Superintendent of the U. S. Life-Saving Service from 1871 through 1914. He was in large measure responsible for the outstanding reputation that the service held.

The first self-righting and self-bailing lifeboat owned by the Coast Guard. It was purchased from the Royal Lifeboat Society of England in 1872. The boat was evaluated in this country and its design served as the basis for the linage of U. S. self-righting, self-bailing lifeboats. This 1872 boat has been preserved and is on display at The Mariners Museum in Newport News, Virginia. ►

A bill passed on Dec. 14, 1854 providing for additional stations on Long Island and New Jersey and a salary of $200 a year for keepers. This was a paltry sum of money even for those days.

It wasn't until about 1880 that the federal government's stations were properly run. It was then that fishermen and others familiar with the coasts were recruited. A former Revenue Marine officer named Sumner Increase Kimball was largely responsible for reorganizing and improving the Life-Saving Service. Kimball came into the Service in 1871 and headed the organization until its merger with

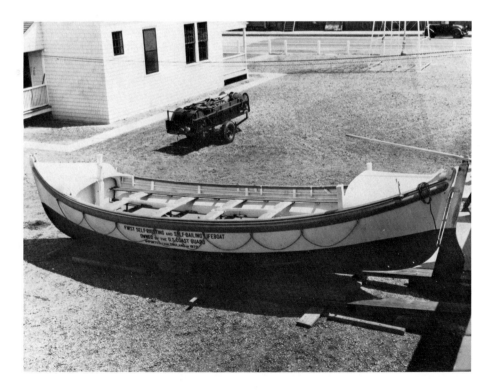

the Revenue Marine in 1915.

Kimball had more of an effect on the operations of the Life-Saving Service than any other individual. But, perhaps the greatest lifesaver of all time was a man whose career began in the volunteer Massachusetts Humane Society and ended in the U.S. Life-Saving Service. His name was Joshua James. James joined the Massachusetts Humane Society in 1842 at the age of 15. He died on duty 60 years later as the keeper of the U.S. Life-Saving Service station at Stony Beach, Massachusetts.

James was the ninth of 12 children. His interest in lifesaving may have developed at the age of 10 after his mother and baby sister died in the sinking of the schooner HEPZIBAH. He started going to sea as a boy with his father and brothers, and then earned his living in the family's shipping business until the age of 62, when he received his appointment to the U.S. Life-Saving Service. James was 17 years past the maximum age limit when he received this appointment, but because of his reputation he was given a waiver.

James was a natural sailor, and the stories about his sailing ability are almost as interesting as his rescues. On one night while underway, the helmsman lost his bearings and James was roused out of bed. He scanned the heavens, set a course, and told the helmsman he would spot a light in two hours. James then went back to sleep. One hour and 55 minutes later, the light was sighted.

On another occasion, he was sailing a yacht in dense fog, and someone asked him where they were. James replied "We are just off Long

◄ *(Left)* **This photograph printed from a broken glass negative reveals the character of the men who served in the Life-Saving Service. The man wearing the double-breasted coat is the keeper.**

◄ *(Right)* **Crew at North Manitou Island Life-Saving Station, Michigan in 1902. Records show the Keeper as Telesford St. Peter.**

◄ **If the wreck was located some distance from the lifesaving station, the boat had to be pulled to the site. Initially manpower was used to get the boats to the site of the disaster. By the late 19th century horses were employed and later still, tractors.**

Early U. S. Life-Saving Station in Chicago, Illinois, circa 1889. ►

Island head." "How can you tell that?" he was asked. "I can hear the land talk," he replied.

James and his crew carried out many famous rescues, but the most outstanding occurred on Nov. 25 and 26, 1888 during one of the worst storms in recorded history. Violent seas were pounding several schooners,

and James and his men went to work. They began by removing nine men from the beached COX AND GREEN with a breeches buoy. They then went after the GERTRUDE ABBOTT eight miles up the beach. It was dark by the time the lifesavers reached the vessel, and a rescue by lifeboat was the only

way of saving the doomed crew. The seas were so rough that James asked for volunteers from his volunteer crew. They all stepped forward.

On their way to the schooner, two men were kept busy bailing out the boat. When they reached the vessel eight crewmen dropped one by one into the outstretched arms of the lifesavers. Then came the hard part — getting back to shore. Two hundred yards from the beach the boat struck a boulder and rolled under water, but the crewmen shifted their weight and saved the lifeboat. Then a monstrous wave lifted the boat and

▼ Rugged crew with surfboats ready for emergency at the U. S. Life-Saving Station, Salisbury Beach, Massachusetts, circa 1900.

Oswego, New York, ► U. S. Life-Saving Station, circa 1912. Great Lakes crews experimented with uniforms during the early days of the service.

▼ Crew wearing cork lifesaving belts launching a surfboat at Orleans Life-Saving Station, Massachusetts in 1908. Kapok was recommended for lifejackets that same year.

smashed it on the rocks. A crowd of people, who had gathered on the beach, rushed into the surf and helped them all to safety.

James and his men then got another lifeboat and went after the other schooners. They rescued crewmen from the BERTHA F. WALKER and the H.C. HIGGINSON under terrible conditions. During the entire 24-hour marathon rescue, they saved 29 people.

The turbulent waters of North Carolina's Outer Banks have also been the site of many shipwrecks and dramatic rescues. The Outer Banks is an 80-mile long sandbar that parallels the North Carolina Coast. At its widest point it is only a couple of miles across, but there is a lot of Coast Guard history surrounding this narrow stretch of

beach and much of it is centered around the Midgett family.

The first Midgett to work for the Coast Guard was L. Barrister Midgett. He was appointed keeper of a U.S. Life-Saving Service station in 1874. Since then hundreds of Midgetts have served in the Coast Guard, the Life-Saving Service, the Lighthouse Service and the Revenue Cutter Service. Seven Midgetts have won Gold Life-Saving Medals and three have won Silver Lifesaving Medals.

Surfman Rasmus S. Midgett won a Gold Life-Saving Medal for a rescue that occurred in August 1899. The barkentine PRISCILLA was driven by 100-mile-an-hour winds into the the shore near the Gull Shoal Life-Saving station. Midgett spotted flotsam during an early morning patrol and heard the cries of the desperate crewmen.

◄ He's the stuff the station crews are made of, this sea-battered Coast Guardsman. Let's leave him nameless, as a picture of the indomitable spirit and courage that carries Coast Guardsmen out to the sea in their little craft through tempest and blizzard on their missions of mercy and rescue.

(Left) **Leroy Midgett** ▶
BM1/c, 26 years of service stationed at Nags Head, received the Gold Lifesaving Medal. He is a cousin of Dan B. Midgett. Midgett is wearing the Gold Lifesaving, Valor, British Medal for ''Gallantry and Humanity'', and Victory Medal.

(Right) **Nelson Midgett,** ▶
Chief Machinist's Mate (CMM), stands atop a motor lifeboat at Coast Guard Lifeboat Station, Oregon Inlet, North Carolina. This photo was taken during World War II, at which time he had 25 years of service in the Coast Guard. He was second in command of the station, and was stationed there for 22 years. His grandfather and Dewey Midgett's grandfather were brothers. (Dewey with 21 years of service was at this time in command of the Coast Guard Life-boat Station at Bodie Island, North Carolina.) Nelson's brother Clarence had retired with 30 years of service, and his brother Jarvis retired with 26 years of Coast Guard service.

Launching Life
Boat
Michigan City

UNITED STATES LIFE SAVING STATION

COPYRIGHT
1906
E. C. CALVERT

◄ **Launching of a surf-boat was an exciting event at the Michigan City, Indiana, Life-Saving Station in 1906.**

One of the most ► **famous lifesavers was Joshua James of Massachusetts. He won numerous life-saving medals from both federal and state governments. At his death in 1902, at the age of 75, a surfboat was used as his coffin. A funeral cortege formed by his family and the crew of the Point Allerton Life-Saving Station rode in a horse-drawn lifeboat.**

Midgett found the ship broken in two with survivors clinging to the wreckage. Instead of making the three-mile trip back to the station, Midgett decided he had to act quickly. He plunged into the rough surf and went after the crewmen. When he reached the PRISCILLA, Midgett ordered each man to jump one at a time into the surf. He then dragged each man to safety.

He did this for 7 of the 10 crewmen. The remaining 3 were too weak to leave the ship. Midgett struggled to the vessel and carried each crewman to the shore.

The U.S. Life-Saving Service had a short but colorful history. It existed for only 44 years before merging with the Revenue Marine in 1915. During this period, 28,121 vessels and 178,741 people were helped by the service. Only 1,455 people lost their lives while exposed to Life-Saving Service rescue operations.

One of the benefits of the 1915 merger was that it solved a major personnel problem for the Life-Saving Service. Before the merger, there had been no retirement system or way of compensating injured crewmen. Salaries were also so low that the organization had trouble attracting young men. There were instances of men in their sixties and seventies manning the boats. The merger created a retirement system for the older keepers and surfmen and also for Sumner I. Kimball as well.

◄ **This early "E" class powered lifeboat kept a full suit of sails and oars on board as well. This lifeboat is being manned by crew from Barnegat Life-Saving Station, New Jersey, circa 1918.**

Whether it be a boat-house ramp launching (right) **or a launching from a two-wheel trailer** (below), **both had to be done with precision and speed since they often meant the difference between life and death.**

Although this might ▶ appear to be a regatta gathering, in fact during the 1920s and '30s it was common practice to draw motor lifeboats and surfboats from Life-Saving Stations throughout the United States to use in the Mississippi River valley for flood relief.

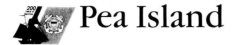

Pea Island

The North Carolina Coast was the site of the Coast Guard's only all-black life-saving station. The station crew was formed at Pea Island because of a scandal. Pea Island had been manned by whites until one of the surfmen failed to notice a ship going aground. Four men died in the breakers, and the station keeper filed a false report about the incident. His deception was discovered. Three people were dismissed and the rest of the crewmen were moved to other stations.

Charles Shoemaker, the investigating officer, recommended that Richard Etheridge, a black man, be the new keeper. He described Etheridge as "strong, intelligent, able to read and write, and one of the best surfmen on this part of the coast of North Carolina."

Etheridge was appointed keeper on Jan. 24, 1880. Within a year arsonists burned his station to the ground. The crew rebuilt it and went about the business of saving lives. Etheridge was a tough man to work for. He drilled his men constantly and made them adhere to strict standards of appearance. The hard work paid off. The station gained a reputation for being the sharpest and best in the district.

"We knew we were colored and, if you know what I mean, felt we had to do better whether anyone said so or not." said William Simmons, a surfman who served at the station during the 1920s.

The men at Pea Island distinguished themselves for the 67 years they operated the station. One of their most dramatic rescues occurred on Oct. 11, 1896. The three-masted schooner E. S. NEWMAN was caught in a winter storm and was breaking up. On board was Captain S.A. Gardiner, his wife, three-year-old daughter and a crew of six.

Gardiner grounded his boat two miles south of the Pea Island station and fired his signal. Ashore, Surfman Theodore Meekins in the Pea Island lookout tower spotted the flare.

The pounding waves were so deadly that Etheridge had suspended the normal foot patrols. The beaches were awash and he feared he would lose one of his men.

Yet when Etheridge heard there was a boat in trouble, he quickly gathered six of his men. With the help of two mules, they dragged their heavy lifesaving equipment across the sand and through the icy water. When they were within shooting distance of the sinking schooner, they found the ground wasn't solid enough to hold the Lyle gun's anchor.

Undaunted, Etheridge tied ropes around his two strongest men and had them swim out to the schooner. The lifesavers secured the line and swam back to shore with Captain Gardiner's three-year-old daughter. They then repeated the trip until all nine passengers were rescued.

◄ A 25-foot, 6-inch self-bailing pulling surfboat is manned by the crew of U. S. Coast Guard Lifeboat Station, Little Creek, Virginia, circa 1940. Little Creek Station, located eight and a half miles west of Cape Henry Light, was built in 1937.

◄ **Lonnie C. Gray, BM1/c blinks signals from the lookout tower at Pea Island to identify friendly craft.**

◄ **Pea Island Life-Saving Station off the coast of North Carolina, photographed here during World War II.**

Crewmen of the all- ► **Black Coast Guard Lifeboat Station at Pea Island, ready a surfboat for launching. Located between Cape Hatteras and Norfolk, the crew was kept busy during World War II watching for trouble from the sea and aiding men in distress. It was no easy task to pull the heavy surfboat to the edge of the beach on the tireless hard-rimmed four-wheel wagon.**

◄ **Photographed during World War II are some of the crew members of the Coast Guard Lifeboat Station at Pea Island, North Carolina. The station was established by an Act of Congress on June 18, 1878, and was built during the winter of 1878-79. Though first manned by whites, it was entirely manned by blacks from 1880 until the station was closed in 1947. The area subsequently became a wildlife refuge. From left to right are Maxie M. Berry, Boatswains Mate 1/c (Officer in Charge), who served 25 years at Pea Island retiring as a Chief Boatswains Mate; Lonnie C. Gray, Boatswains Mate 1/c; Ruben Gallop, Surfman; Fleetwood M. Dunston, Surfman; and Herbert M. Collins, Surfman, who became an expert instructor in boat handling, and retired as a Lieutenant on August 1, 1973.**

(Inset) **Using a marine ► railway the Neah Bay, Washington, Life-Saving crew stands ready to launch their surf boat.**

Another tool of the Life-Saving Service was the self-bailing, self-righting lifeboat. This boat was large and much heavier than the surfboat, thus not suited to all stations. Although this type boat could be launched through the surf, this in fact was not practical. Lifeboats were most commonly found at stations where marine railways could be built. These were ramps fitted with tracks designed to accommodate the heavier boats. In order to have a marine railway you need access to a launching site with deep water. For this reason, self-bailing, self-righting motor lifeboats were usually employed in harbors and on the Great Lakes and Pacific Coast.

◄ *(Left)* **Crew of the Willapa Bay U. S. Life-Saving Station practices with the breeches buoy equipment. This rescue device allowed a strong line to be stretched between the shore and a ship wreck near the beach. Once the line was established, those in distress could be pulled to safety. In this practice, the lifesavers are aiming at a drill pole in the left of the photograph.**

◄ *(Right)* **Surfmen with shoulder lines pulling a beach cart equipped with a Lyle gun and breeches buoy rescue apparatus at the U. S. Life-Saving Station at Salisbury Beach, Massachusetts, circa 1900. The Lyle gun was used to throw the shot, to which a rescue line was attached, to the distressed vessel** *(right).*

◄ **Horsepower helps manpower drag a surfboat from the sea, Orleans Life-Saving Station, Massachusetts, circa 1908.**

Breeches buoy
at work. ▶

◄ Over the chasm
between two ships in
the mid-Atlantic, an ail-
ing merchant seaman is
transferred by breeches
buoy from his ship to a
Coast Guard combat
cutter for medical treat-
ment. The buoy is used
when the launching of
small boats is deemed
inadvisable.

"Special Delivery" ►
to the doctor over a sea
churning angrily, an ail-
ing Coast Guardsman is
whisked via stokes lit-
ter to another ship for
surgical treatment. Be-
hind him along the line,
linking the two ships,
tags a bag of his per-
sonal belongings.

U.S. COAST GUARD

◄ **The first rescue motor surfboat powered by gas turbine is shown here. It is 26 feet long, and constructed of fiberglass-reinforced plastic and fire-retardant polyester. Designed with an eye for traditional ruggedness, the new 26-footer is an advanced modification of a type of small self-bailing, nonsinkable rescue craft. This boat was first unveiled in February, 1963.**

◄ *(Inset)* **Self-bailing, self-righting lifeboat of the Coast Guard, with sails set, performing boat drill.**

Steamboat Inspection Service & Navigation Bureau

When steamboats first came into use, a voyage on one of those early mechanical marvels was a very risky trip. They were constantly blowing up. There were many problems with the design and improper use of boilers. Early boilers were square and could not resist high pressures. Seawater was also used which quickly rusted the metal and built up dangerous mineral deposits.

The Steamboat Inspection Service and the Bureau of Navigation were both formed in the mid-19th century after a series of spectacular steamboat explosions and navigation accidents. These two organizations merged in 1932 before joining the Coast Guard in 1946. They were the predecessors of today's Coast Guard regulatory functions.

The explosion of the steamboat PULASKI off North Carolina in 1837 triggered the federal government's involvement in streamboat regulation. The next year the regulation of steamboats began in earnest. Skilled engineers were required, hulls and boilers were inspected, and the vessels had to be equipped with lifeboats, fire pumps, hoses, signal lights and other safety equipment.

This was the birth of commercial vessel safety. Unfortunately, the rules were not enforced as well as they should have been. District judges appointed local people as inspectors, and many of the inspectors had close ties to the industry. Also, there were no universal safety standards.

The steamboats kept blowing up. From December 1851 through July of the next year, nearly 700 people were killed in seven major disasters. Congress responded by passing The Steamboat Act in 1852. This provided for nine supervising inspectors who were experts in construction and operation of commercial vessels. They met once a year and drew up new regulations.

The board faced its greatest challenge shortly after the turn of the century. On June 15th, 1904 the excursion steamer GENERAL SLOCUM burned in the East River with the loss of 957 lives, many of whom were school children on a church excursion from one parish. The Steamboat Inspection Service received much of the blame for the disaster. After the accident Congress gave the board additional authority to create fire prevention and extinguishing rules and prescribe lifesaving equipment.

The steamer ▶
GENERAL SLOCUM
burned in the East River
with the loss of 957
lives.

◀ **Fire aboard the**
MORRO CASTLE had the
biggest impact on mari-
time safety in U. S.
history.

THE
SECOND
CENTURY

The Twentieth Century

When the Civil War ended in 1865, the country entered a period of explosive boom-and-bust growth, sparked, in large part, by new inventions. From the Coast Guard's birthday in 1790 to 1860 there were 36,000 patents filed in America. From 1860 to 1900, 640,000 patents were filed. This inventive trend continued in the 20th century and the Coast Guard was involved in a number of interesting firsts.

In 1903, members of the Kill Devil Hills Life-Saving Station helped usher in the age of flight when they gave the Wright brothers' plane a push at Kitty Hawk, N.C. Keeper J.T. Daniels had the dubious distinction of being the first person injured in an airplane accident. Right after the Wright brothers' 12-second flight, their flimsy airplane was hit by a gust of wind and began to flip over. Daniels and the others tried to steady the plane but failed. The machine rolled over and over with the tenacious Daniels holding on. He was dragged along the beach and was pitched head-over-heels into the airplane.

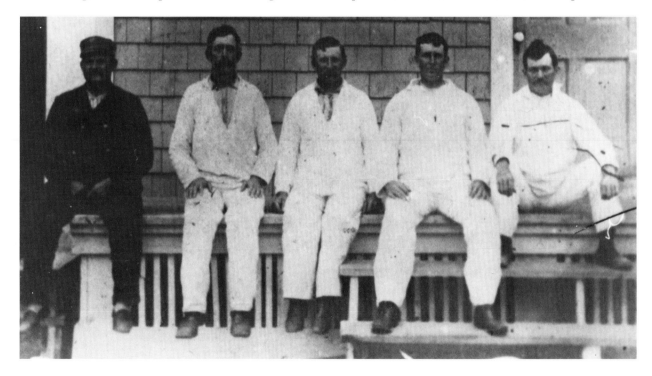

Coast Guardsmen of the Kill Devil Hills Life-Saving Station who assisted with the Wright brothers first flight. Left to right are Ward, William Thomas Beacham, ?, John T. Daniels, and W. S. Dough. They helped move the aircraft from its hanger to Kill Devil Kill.

Daniels was badly bruised when he hit the machinery but was not seriously injured.

Another first occurred in 1905. An experimentally installed radio on the lightship NANTUCKET helped save the cutter's crew. During a severe gale, the lightship sprung a leak and began to sink. The SOS distress signal was not in use at the time, so the radio operator kept spelling the word "help" in both the international and American Morse codes. The message was received and the lighthouse tender AZALEA braved the storm to rescue the lightship. The tender took the lightship in tow, but the NANTUCKET was too badly damaged, it sank on its way to New Bedford. There was no loss of life.

On Jan. 23, 1909, the revenue cutter SENECA made history when it responded to the world's first SOS. It came from Jack Binns, the radio operator of the steamship REPUBLIC. The vessel had collided with the FLORIDA and was sinking. The SENECA picked up the distress call and raced to assist the REPUBLIC. The cutter arrived on scene shortly after the revenue cutter GRESHAM. The GRESHAM picked up the crew before the REPUBLIC sank.

On the night of April 14, 1912, a distress call

◄ **The luxury liner TITANIC departs Southampton, England, prior to her maiden voyage.**

from the wireless of another vessel shocked the world and changed the Coast Guard. The "unsinkable" TITANIC hit an iceberg on her maiden voyage and went to the bottom of the North Atlantic. More than 1,500 passengers and crewmen died.

There had been several other terrible losses caused by North Atlantic icebergs, but the TITANIC's sinking moved the maritime nations to action. The U.S. Navy patrolled for icebergs during the rest of the season and beginning in 1913 the revenue cutters SENECA and MIAMI and the British trawler SCOTIA assumed the duty.

A North Atlantic ice patrol was established at the International Conference on the Safety of Life at Sea in London in 1914. The United States was designated to maintain the patrol and several European nations would help pay for the service.

The Revenue Cutter Service was selected to do the job. Since then, the Coast Guard has patrolled for icebergs during every ice season with the exception of the two world wars. Not a single ship has been lost to ice within the patrolled area while the patrols were being carried out. The cutters originally assigned to the patrols have been replaced by HC-130 aircraft.

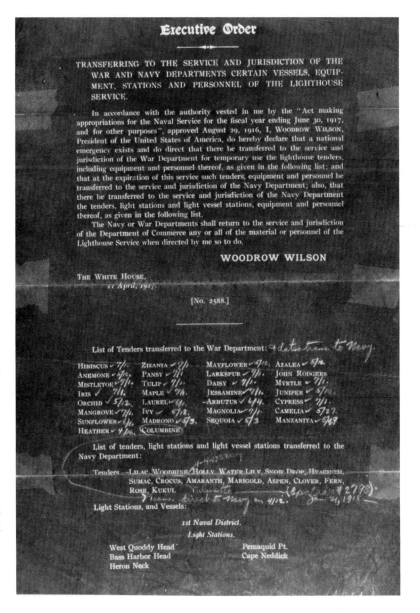

◄ **A new TAMPA (WPG-48) was commissioned on September 15, 1921. Shown here is the crew of the TAMPA in Mobile, Alabama, 1929.**

World War I

In 1915 the name, United States Coast Guard, came into being when the Revenue Cutter Service and the Life-Saving Service merged. World War I had begun one year earlier. The United States did not enter the war until 1917, but the U.S. Lighthouse Service's lightships were involved before that date.

German U-boats attacked ships in the North Atlantic in an effort to stop supplies from reaching Britain. One favorite submarine lair was near the NANTUCKET lightship. In one raid U-53 sank several unarmed merchant ships and the crews took refuge on the lightship. At one time there were 115 shipwrecked men aboard the lightship and 19 ships' boats trailing astern. All the sailors were brought safely to land.

When the United States entered the war, the newly formed Coast Guard was once again thrown into battle. Six hours after President Woodrow Wilson approved the Declaration of War on April 6, 1917, the Coast Guard's 47 vessels and 279 shore stations were at the service of the Navy.

Coast Guardsmen suffered the highest proportion of casualties of all U.S. armed forces during World War I as they carried out their main mission of convoying merchant ships between Gibraltar and Great Britain.

The cutter TAMPA was the worst Coast Guard loss. On the night of Sept. 26, 1918, the TAMPA was heading to Wales after escorting a convoy into the safety of Bristol Channel.

Genevieve and ►
Lucille Baker, 19-year-old twins, were the first women to serve in the new Coast Guard during World War I.

◄ **Cutter TAMPA was sunk by a German submarine 26 September 1918, with all hands. This was the largest individual naval loss sustained during World War I, with the exception of the collier CYCLOPS.**

A torpedo destroyed the cutter and killed all 115 men, 111 of whom were Coast Guardsmen. A few pieces of wreckage and two unidentified bodies were all that was found.

The 199 Coast Guard stations on the Atlantic and Gulf Coast also kept an alert eye out for survivors of U-boat attacks. The saving of most of the crew of the British tanker MIRLO on the afternoon of Aug. 16, 1918, was one of the most dramatic rescues. The sound of an explosion and a cloud of smoke alerted Keeper John A. Midgett and his crew at Station Chicamacomico, N.C. to the torpedo attack about seven miles offshore.

The men rushed to their surfboats and headed for the vessel. About five miles from shore they met the captain and six of the crew in a lifeboat. Midgett was told that two other lifeboats had managed to get off, but that one of them had capsized near the tanker.

Midgett told the Englishman to wait for him to return and not attempt to land through the surf. He then went after the two boats. The seas were covered with burning oil for hundreds of yards around the sinking tanker. When the smoke cleared, Midgett saw an overturned lifeboat with six men clinging to it between two burning walls of oil. He skillfully guided his boat through the wreckage and picked up the survivors.

A descendant of ► John A. Midgett is seen here on June 15, 1952, clipping the station mascot at Chicamacomico, North Carolina.

Sixteen men were originally clinging to the overturned lifeboat but between fighting the flames and water 10 died before the lifesavers reached them. Midgett then located the other boat with 20 men on board and took it in tow. He returned to the boat at anchor and successfully landed all of the men. Midgett and his crew saved 36 lives.

Coast Guard pilots also played a role in World War I. Coast Guard aviation has a very long history; it dates back to 1916. This is only 13 years after Keeper Daniels and his men gave the Wright brothers' plane a push at Kitty Hawk, N.C.

The air wing began in April 1916, when six Coast Guard pilots were assigned to the Naval Aviation School in Pensacola, Fla. They were accepted into Pensacola after Lieutenants Elmer Stone and Norman Hall demonstrated that the airplane had a place in the Coast Guard.

Stone and Hall had borrowed a Curtis Flying Boat from the Curtis Flying School at Newport News, Va. and flew experimental flights offshore. They never ventured beyond sight of land, because the plane lacked navigation equipment, but their efforts were enough to get them into flight school.

The six Pensacola trained Coast Guard pilots were absorbed into the Navy's aviation wing during World War I where they served with distinction. They were assigned to naval air stations in this country and abroad. One Coast Guardsman commanded the Naval Air Station, Ille Tudy, France, and won the French "Chevalier of the Legion of Honor". Another commanded the Chatham Naval Air Station.

▼ **Elmer F. Stone, the first Coast Guard aviator and pioneer in the use of aircraft for rescue and patrol work.**

The late RADM Norman B. Hall, USCG, pioneer ►
in U. S. Coast Guard Aviation, is pictured second
from left with a Curtis crew in 1916, when he was
stationed at the Curtis Aircraft plant. RADM Hall
used a Curtis H-10 plane in developing aero-
navigations systems in 1916. He was a 2nd
Lieutenant of Engineers at this time.

▼ The first Coast Guard
aviation group was
trained at the Naval Air
Station, Pensacola,
Florida, during 1916-17.

Post-World War I

After the war, the development of the Coast Guard's air wing was put on hold. There was, however, one notable aviation achievement. Lieutenant Stone made aviation history as one of the pilots who flew the first aircraft across the Atlantic Ocean.

At that time, the English and the Americans were competing to be the first to fly across the Atlantic. On the morning of May 17, 1919, three U.S. Navy seaplanes, the NC-1, NC-3 and the NC-4, went after the record.

The planes had a 126-foot wing span and carried a crew of five: a commanding officer, two pilots, a radioman and an engineer. Lt. Stone was one of the pilots of the NC-4. Instead of flying directly for Europe the planes attempted to make the trip in several hops. The first would be Newfoundland, the second the Azores, then the continent and finally the British Isles.

The day after they took off, the NC-1 was forced to put down in the ocean and sank, but the crew was rescued. The NC-3 also put down in the water and her crew was rescued two days later. Only the NC-4 made it to the Azores and two weeks later it finished the flight to Plymouth, England.

The stalling of the development of Coast Guard aviation was the least of the service's problems in the early 20s. The Coast Guard's very identity was being questioned.

The Coast Guard had changed dramatically only a few years earlier when the Revenue Cutter Service and the Life-Saving Service merged. For almost half of that time the Coast Guard had served under the Navy. The Coast Guard's officer corps felt more of a kinship with U.S. Navy officers than with their new colleagues from the Life-Saving Service. The majority of the officers wanted the Coast Guard to remain in the Navy instead of moving it back into the Treasury Department. This would have ended the existence of the Coast Guard as a separate service. Several congressmen were opposed to keeping the Coast Guard in the Navy and the service reverted back to the Treasury Department.

On the enlisted side there were also problems. Most of the men, who had volunteered for service during the war, now wanted to be discharged. In the early 20s the service had only three-fifths of its authorized enlisted strength.

The Coast Guard stumbled along, undermanned and in need of new cutters. But it did manage to perform competently as revealed by statistics from *annual reports*.

◄ **NC-4 in the harbor at Lisbon, Portugal, after arrival on May 27, 1919, completing the first successful flight across the Atlantic on the fifth leg of its journey. Lieutenant Elmer Stone successfully piloted the plane.**

Fiscal Year	Lives Saved	People Assisted	Vessels Seized or Reported for Violating Laws
1919	2,081	12,044	152
1920	2,417	8,424	601
1921	1,621	14,013	340
1922	2,954	14,531	596
1923	2,792	16,253	2,106
1924	2,462	15,902	2,205

The most dramatic statistical jump was in the number of vessels seized or reported for violating laws in 1923. This was because of the passage of the 18th Amendment to the Constitution on Jan. 16, 1920. This new amendment outlawed the sale of liquor.

▼ Among the cruising cutters available at the onset of Prohibition were former U. S. Navy Eagle Boats.

The Prohibition Years

Prohibition lasted from 1920 until the amendment was repealed in 1933. The Coast Guard reached new lows in public opinion during those years. Many Americans were against Prohibition, and they resented the Coast Guard's efforts to stop the flow of liquor.

In the beginning, the tiny Coast Guard fleet was swamped by the smugglers. Liquor-laden boats hovered off the coast of the United States and ran their cargoes into the harbors more or less at will. These "rum rows" were permanent fixtures of many American cities.

The service slowly got involved in enforcing the new law and then underwent a quick expansion. When the Coast Guard hit the rum-runners harder the service faced increased criticism from the public, the press and even foreign governments.

One of the worst incidents occurred when

▼ **Cutter DEXTER, July, 1933.**

officer-in-charge Boatswain A.W. Powell of the cutter DEXTER sank the Canadian-registered I'M ALONE in international waters after the vessel refused to stop to be boarded. The captain of the I'M ALONE died in the incident and the Canadian, French and British governments protested the Coast Guard's action. The United States compensated the Canadian government and the victims even though the I'M ALONE was smuggling and was first spotted within the 12-mile limit of the United States.

Rum Schooner, former fisherman, Henry L. Marshall, McCoy's first vessel in the bootlegging business. She was under another skipper when captured in 1921. McCoy saw the possibility of quick money in supplying "high grade" liquor to eager, high-paying customers.

Nine months after the sinking of the I'M ALONE, the Coast Guard was once again under attack over an incident involving the rum-runner BLACK DUCK.

The BLACK DUCK had been caught sneaking into Narragansett Bay, Rhode Island by Boatswain Alexander C. Cornell, the officer-in-charge of CG 290. When the vessel tried to flee, Cornell ordered his gunner to fire nearby. The BLACK DUCK turned as the gunner fired and the bullets crashed into the pilot house. The rum-runner disappeared into the fog. Shortly thereafter it reappeared and bumped into the patrol boat.

Three men were killed and a fourth wounded by the gunner. The public's displeasure with the Coast Guard spread throughout New England. It was so bad for a while that recruiting had to be stopped in Boston and Coast Guardsmen on liberty in

The crew of the ▶
cutter SNOHOMISH
pose for a photograph
in 1923. This crew was
involved in the war on
smugglers in the Pacific
Northwest.

Contraband runner
78-foot, two-masted
lumber schooner Mary
Langdon of Rockland,
Maine, is flanked by the
U. S. Coast Guard cutter
Redwing (left) and
75-foot patrol boat
CG-237 after she was
seized on June 10,
1925, and towed into
New Bedford, Massa-
chusetts. The schooner
carried 2,000 cases of
Scotch whiskey in her
holds (following page).

▼ **Two "six bitters" stop a rum runner on the high seas. The Coast Guard constructed over 200 of these sturdy craft. This was the largest class of cutters built by the Coast Guard until the advent of World War II.**

New London, Conn. were attacked.

There was less public outcry when Coast Guardsmen were killed. In one incident, Chief Boatswains Mate Sydney Sanderlin, Machinist Mate Victor Lamby, and Secret Service Agent Robert Webster were killed in a gun battle with smugglers while aboard the patrol boat, CG 249. The rum-runners were eventually caught. One of them turned state's evidence and was sentenced to a year and a day in prison. The other was

hanged at the Coast Guard Base at Fort Lauderdale, Fla.

The repeal of Prohibition took the profit out of smuggling liquor, but not out of smuggling. The smugglers turned to other sources of revenue. They ran guns to Central American countries and returned with German narcotics. They also smuggled illegal aliens into the United States. This continued until the beginning of World War II and kept the Coast Guard busy.

Crew of CG-158 looks over a stash of illegal liquor which they had recently seized. Note that the liquor is packaged in burlap sacks. This was done to facilitate the loading and unloading by the rum-runners. The single shot six-pounder just forward of the bridge was the principal weapon mounted on the "six bitters."

Throughout Coast Guard history, even during the low points, such as prohibition, there have been some amusing and unusual stories. One of these involved a wandering buoy.

Frying Pan Shoal buoy 2A FP broke away from its mooring off the North Carolina coast and took off. The buoy was big and expensive, and the Coast Guard wanted it back.

But the buoy drifted into the Gulf Steam and sailed away to Europe. Ten times the buoy was sighted and reported but all attempts to recover it failed. Finally after a 4,000 mile voyage, it landed in County Cork, Ireland. The buoy had been at sea for one year and one month.

Its odyssey was the subject of a poem in the Saturday Evening Post:

> *Now when and why, and how came he*
> *To slip his mooring and put to sea*
> *With an impudent whistle and lazy roll?*
> *Fool, to be bound when he might be free!*
> *Was it a choice to be pondered o'er. . .*
>
> *Weeks and months did he roll at will,*
>
> *For they found him all spent on the Irish stand*
> *And they seized him and put him in chains once more,*
>
> *Whose dull life palled, and who longed to be free,*
> *And defied the world and went off to sea.*

Coast Guard Aviation

In the 30s, the air wing of the Coast Guard came into its own. The first purchase of planes was in 1926, when five aircraft were bought to help enforce Prohibition, but little else was done until the early 30s.

The service then bought several planes, and others were transferred from the Navy and the Customs Service. The transferred planes were a mixed blessing. The fabric on one of the Navy aircraft was so bad that the plane was stripped and re-covered by the Coast Guardsmen and their wives. Many of the contributions from Customs were also in poor shape. Several crashed shortly after they were turned over to the Coast Guard.

The purchase of seven "flying lifeboats" in 1932 put the air wing solidly into the search and rescue business. These amphibians were designed to land on the water in rough seas and pick up survivors.

By 1936 the Coast Guard had six air stations, two air detachments and 42 aircraft. The service also began putting aircraft on cutters in the 30s. The 327-foot cutters carried Grumman JF-2 amphibians. The planes and cutters searched for opium smugglers, enforced fisheries laws in the Pacific, and patrolled the Atlantic to protect the new transcontinental commercial air service.

The late 30s were dynamic years for the

▼ **The first airplane constructed for the U. S. Coast Guard Air Service, a Loening Amphibian, Model OL-5 No. 1, was delivered on October, 1926.**

**The Coast Guard ▶
commissioned two
Chance-Vought-UO-4s
in December 1926.
They had a top speed
of 106 knots.**

Coast Guard. Along with the developments in aviation, the size of the fleet increased. The service also began training merchant seaman and became more involved in boating safety. The latter task was assigned to the Coast Guard Auxiliary, which was formed on June 23, 1939.

The service also absorbed the U.S. Lighthouse Service on July 1, 1939. This was a difficult pill to swallow. A military organization of 10,164 people had to take 4,119 full-time and 1,156 part-time civilian employees. Many people in the Lighthouse Service didn't want anything to do with the military. They were members of the country's oldest government service and had a long and honorable history. Their 250th anniversary was due a couple of months after the merger announcement.

The Coast Guard handled the merger as best it could. Lighthouse employees who wished to remain civilians were allowed to do so, others were given military ranks. Lighthouse keepers became either chiefs or first class petty officers, junior officers from the Lighthouse Service's fleet of tenders were offered warrant appointments and most of the tender captains and chief engineers were commissioned chief boatswains and chief machinists.

Crew members preparing to launch a Grumman JF-2, the "Duck." With the help of the boat crane the plane is picked up from the cradle and lowered over the side, and from there the take off.

(Top left) **An N4Y-1 used by the Coast Guard from 1932-40s.**

(Top right) **Manufactured in 1934 by Vought, and put into service in 1935 by the Coast Guard. This aircraft was used briefly for patrolling the Mexican boarder for aliens, and later the Canadian border of rum runners.**

(Middle left) **RD-4 was used from 1934-43 by the Coast Guard.**

(Middle right) **JF-2, manufactured by Grumman, but better known as the ''Duck'', was put into service in 1934.**

(Bottom left) **The R3Q-1 ''Reliant'' operated out of Cape May, New Jersey in 1937.**

(Bottom right) **RT-1, Delta, an eight-place passenger transport version of the Gamma, was used between 1935-40. The RT-1 was nicknamed the Golden Goose in 1939, and was the official transport plane of Secretary of Treasury Henry Morgenthau, Jr. The Secretary championed the development of Coast Guard aviation.**

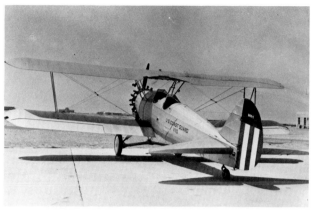

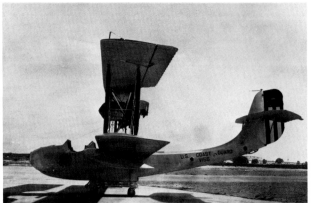

(Top left) **One Lockheed R30-1 was purchased by the Coast Guard and used for ten years from 1936-46.**

(Top right) **This Viking 00-1 was one of five used by the Coast Guard from 1936-41.**

(Middle left) **J2K-2 was used from 1937-41.**

(Middle right) **The PH-2, built in 1938, had a take-off time of less than 20 seconds in calm weather. The Coast Guard Magazine reported that Lieutenant Carl B. Olsen lifted the V-164 off the water in five seconds during take-off performance tests.**

(Bottom left) **The Grumman Goose was used from 1939-47.**

(Bottom right) **The Curtiss SOC-4 entered service in 1938. Prior to the United States' entry into World War II, the SOC-4 was used off the cutter DUANE to survey the coast of Greenland for potential airfield sites during the summer of 1941.**

Air Station Port Angeles, Washington, was the first Coast Guard Air Station on the West coast. It was placed in commission in 1935.

◄ The first Coast Guard helicopter detachment was headed by the then Lt. Commander Frank A. Erickson, shown here fifth from left. He was the first U. S. Coast Guardsman to qualify as a helicopter pilot, and he pioneered rotary wing development for military use.

◄ Seen here is the Lockheed HC-130B in August, 1977. The Coast Guard received its first HC-130 Hercules in 1959. This aircraft is capable of cruising on two of its four engines, thus greatly extending its range.

The Sikorsky HNS-1 was the first helicopter used by the Coast Guard for search and rescue. Shown here is the HNS-1 hovering with a stretcher suspended below.

The Bell HTL was first put into service in 1947.

The HRP-1 Banana was commissioned in November 1948. It is shown here hovering off the ground at the U. S. Coast Guard Station, Elizabeth City, North Carolina, January 1951.

The Sikorsky HH-3F was put into service in 1969. Shown here is a HH-3F from USCG Station New Orleans over Lake Pontchartrain.

A Sikorsky HH-52A
Seaguard and a 30-foot
utility boat (CG-30526)
team for patrol.

◄ **The cutter NORTH-
LAND made the first
American naval capture
in World War II.**

World War II

Coast Guard involvement in World War II began shortly after the outbreak of the war in Europe. Coast Guardsmen inspected ships to make sure they were not carrying weapons. Port security, and explosives and dangerous cargo handling also became important Coast Guard duties as the war neared.

Coast Guardsmen even took action against interned ships in American harbors.

On March 30, 1941 Coast Guardsmen boarded two German, 26 Italian and 35 Danish vessels and removed their crews after it was reported that Axis sailors were sabotaging the vessels. Many of the ships were later used by the Allies.

Greenland was incorporated into a hemisphere defense system on April 9, 1941, and the Coast Guard evolved into the primary

**The BEAR built in ►
1874, the oldest Coast
Guard cutter to see
duty in World War II
was reconditioned by
the Navy and armed
for duty around
Greenland.**

military service responsible for cold-weather operations. The cutter NORTHLAND made the first American naval capture of World War II in these waters when it took into "protective custody" the Norwegian trawler BESKOE and captured three German radiomen ashore. The Coast Guard played a major role in Greenland throughout the war by stopping the Germans from setting up vital weather stations and providing other essential services.

On Dec. 7, 1941 when the Japanese attacked Pearl Harbor, the Coast Guard Cutter TANEY was in Honolulu Harbor and fired on enemy aircraft. The next day, the Coast Guard suffered its first casualty when the Coast Guard-manned transport LEONARD WOOD was attacked by Japanese aircraft at Singapore.

Throughout the war, Coast Guardsmen did a wide variety of jobs at sea and on the shore. Protecting convoys from enemy submarines was one of their primary missions. Coast Guard-manned ships sank 11 enemy U-boats, and a Coast Guard aircraft was the first plane ever to sink a submarine. The majority of the sinkings occurred in the early years of the war. By mid-1943, U.S. warships had sunk only 11 U-boats; 6 of them were destroyed by Coast Guard cutters. These early sinkings were critical to the American war effort because at the time victory in the "Battle of the Atlantic" was still in doubt.

The manning of amphibious ships and landing craft was another vital Coast Guard mission. Many of the Coast Guardsmen who served on board the 22 Navy transports were former surfmen. They landed soldiers and

◄ The cutter TANEY seen here at Mare Island, California, May 4, 1941.

Marines at every important invasion, and also trained the other military services in the use of landing craft.

Signalman First ►
Class Douglas Munro,
the Coast Guard's first
and only winner of the
Congressional Medal
of Honor.

At Guadalcanal, Signalman First Class Douglas Munro led the rescue of a company of Marines who were about to be overrun by the Japanese. He died after maneuvering his boat between the enemy and the evacuating Marines. For his actions Munro was awarded the Congressional Medal of Honor.

Coast Guard expertise in lifesaving was also put to good use. Coast Guard cutters, boats and aircraft rescued more than 1,500 survivors of submarine attacks near the United States. Coast Guardsmen on escort duty saved an additional 1,000 people and rescued more than 1,500 during the invasion of Normandy.

The sinking of the troopship DORCHESTER

was one of the most tragic as well as dramatic Coast Guard rescue operations. The DORCHESTER was torpedoed on the morning of Feb. 3, 1943. Most of the men on board were thrown into the deadly cold water. The ESCANABA and COMANCHE went to the rescue of the half-frozen sailors and soldiers.

The cutters had to get the men out of the water quickly and also avoid being sunk by an enemy submarine. The Coast Guardsmen tried a new rescue technique. Coast Guardsmen clad in rubber suits and tied to lines were put over the side of the vessel and dragged through the water. They grabbed survivors and secured a line around them. The men were then hauled on board the cutter. When the Coast Guardsman in the water was too exhausted to continue, he was hauled back on board and another man took his place. The ESCANABA saved 132 men and the COMANCHE saved 97 that night, but more than 600 people lost their lives including 16 Coast Guardsmen. Four months after this rescue the 165-foot ESCANABA was torpedoed by a U-boat. The cutter sank within three minutes, 100 men died and only two survived.

Coast Guard picket boats also patrolled for enemy U-boats along the American coast; while on the shore, Coast Guardsmen patrolled beaches and docks. About 24,000 Coast Guardsmen guarded an area of 3,700 miles along the Atlantic, Gulf and Pacific coasts. They used almost 2,000 dogs and 3,200 horses for these patrols.

The beach patrol system developed early in

◄ **Mrs. Edith Munro, mother of Congressional Medal of Honor winner Douglas Munro, was a Lieutenant junior grade in the Coast Guard's Women's Reserve.**

the war, after Seaman John C. Cullen of the Amagansett Station on Long Island, N.Y. encountered four German saboteurs on the night of June 13, 1942 while on patrol. The leader of the group threatened Cullen and then offered him a bribe. Cullen accepted the money and then reported the incident. The next morning several cases of German explosives and detonators were found. The Federal Bureau of Investigation was notified and their agents captured the Germans.

Very early in the war, the Coast Guard was also tasked with developing the helicopter as an anti-submarine tool. As the war progressed, the U-boat threat abated and helicopter development focused on search and rescue. The helicopter's use as a life-saving tool was demonstrated before its anti-submarine capabilities.

When the destroyer TURNER exploded off Sandy Hook, 156 survivors were picked up by Coast Guard craft and rushed to Sandy Hook

Rescue of the crew ▶ of the troopship DORCHESTER on the morning of February 3, 1943.

Members of the ▶
U. S. Coast Guard's
mounted beach patrol
gallop along a wave-
washed beach on the
coast in an early
morning drill.

RECREATION BLDG.
FOR ENLISTED MEN

Beach Patrol Petty Officers School, May 15, 1943, at the Coast Guard base, Portsmouth Navy Yard.

A Coast Guardsman ▶ and his dog patrol a lonely stretch of coastline, alert for suspects who might be enemy spies or saboteurs landing on United States shores from the sea. Dogs proved alert, loyal teammates of Coast Guardsmen on the war-time beach patrol.

(Bottom left) **Coast** ▶ **Guardsman Evans E. Mitchell** gives a pat of thanks to Nora, the eight-months-old shepherd who brought help when she discovered the Coast Guardsman unconscious on the beach at Oregon Inlet, N. C. Mitchell had fainted, while on night patrol, in an isolated spot and was in danger of dying from cold and exposure. A few months earlier a Coast Guardsman from the Oregon Inlet Station had purchased Nora for fifty cents. Her duty far exceeded her worth!!!

(Bottom right) **Captain** ▶ **Raymond J. Mauerman,** former chief training officer of the Coast Guard Dog Patrol, examines a pair of the new canvas boots, worn by Poncho, designed to protect the war dogs' feet from cuts from oyster shells while on long beach patrols.

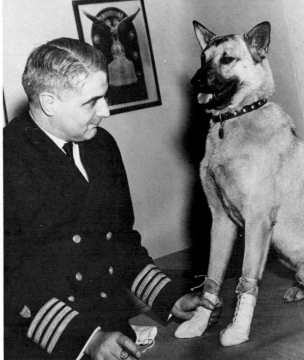

◄ **U. S. Coast Guards-men patrolling an isolated section of the nation's Pacific shore break into a gallop as they hit a stretch of hot sand. Patrols were maintained day and night during war-time.**

(Top left) **Man, dog,** ►
and horse have always been inseparable pals. U. S. Coast Guardsman Joe Opalka, blacksmith at a horse and dog beach patrol station on the Pacific coast, prepares to shoe an equine Coast Guard member, while a canine guardian holds fast the reins.

(Top right) **Seen here is** ►
Captain Frank A. Erickson.

Coast Guard ►
masters and dogs in training for Coast Guard Dog Patrol duty.

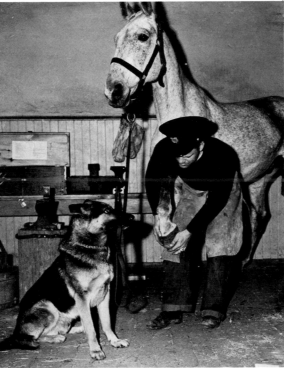

Marching from class at Hunter College, Coast Guard SPARS go through basic training with Waves, circa 1942.

(Top left) **Captain Dorothy C. Stratton, Director of the Coast Guard SPARS, is shown receiving the Legion of Merit Medal from Admiral Joseph F. Farley, Commandant of the Coast Guard.** ▶

(Bottom left) **In May 1944 Miss Dorothy Hayes (seated) of Winston-Salem, North Carolina, signs on the dotted line and becomes a SPAR. Seen here with her are Lieutenant Commander Helen B. Schleman, executive officer of the SPARs from Washington, D. C. (left), and SPAR recruiter Virginia Clark of the Raleigh, North Carolina, recruiting office.** ▶

(Far right) **In Alaska a young Thlinger Indian lad explains the why and wherefore of a totem pole to the first Coast Guard SPAR officer, Lt. Commander Theresa M. Crowley (left) assigned to duty in Alaska, while Commander Helen B. Schleman and Lt. Laura Bevis show interest. Commander Schleman and Lt. Bevis were on temporary duty inspecting quarters for the first group of SPARS to be assigned to Alaska in 1945.** ▶

◄ **The SPAR Glee Club furnished music for the Sunday morning services.**

◄ *(Bottom left)* **Candle-blowing ceremonies in the Third Coast Guard District Office high-lighted the 23rd anniversary of the SPARs. The participants (left to right) are: Renee Dennerlein, SNYN, USCGR; Diane Denny, SNSK, USCGR; Capt. W. B. Ellis, USCG, Third Coast Guard District Chief of Staff; Lt. Commander Mary Bachand, USCGR-R; Capt. G. I. Garner, USCG, Third District Reserve Division Chief; Margaret DelPrado, SNYN, USCGR; and Maureen Thompson, SNYN, USCGR.**

◄ *(Bottom right)* **First class of women reservists to receive basic military training in 25 years. Shown here in August 1972 are the graduates at U. S. Coast Guard Reserve Training Center, Yorktown, Virginia. The class consisted of two groups, of which this is the second, of about 30 each, completing two weeks of indoctrination.**

Debra Lee Wilson, Boatswain's Mate 3/c, splices a tow line at Coast Guard Station, Fort Point, San Francisco, California, where she was assigned as a coxswain of a 44-foot motor lifeboat. BM3 Wilson was one of two women stationed among 25 men at Fort Point.

hospital. Meeting the demands of patients quickly used up the hospital's supply of plasma. Severe snow squalls and sleet had closed all of the air fields in the New York area and Coast Guard Air Station Brooklyn was called upon to fly plasma from Battery Park in Manhattan to Sandy Hook. Commander Frank A. Erickson flew to the Battery through the blinding sleet and show, picked up two cases of plasma and delivered them to the hospital. Because of his actions several sailors were saved.

Coast Guardsmen also guided ships and bombers across the ocean with the newly developed Loran electronic navigation system during the war. Loran was so critical in the

◄ **Proposed uniforms created for Coast Guard women by famous designer Edith Head are test-worn here, November 1974, for the first time by five Coast Guard women at Headquarters.**

Lieutenant (jg) ► Beverly Kelly, seen here on April 30, 1979, was the first woman to ever Command a U. S. military vessel, the 95-foot **USCG CAPE NEWAGEN** based at Maui, Hawaii. This vessel had a crew of 14, and carried out Search and Rescue and Law Enforcement missions.

Pacific theater, that Coast Guardsmen had the Iwo Jima and Okinawa stations on the air before the Japanese were cleared from the islands.

There were many interesting personnel changes during the war, including the introduction of women. About 10,000 women came into the Coast Guard Reserve. The women's auxiliary was organized by Lieu-tenant Dorothy C. Stratton, of the Navy's Women Accepted for Volunteer Emergency Service (WAVES).

She gave the women's auxiliary its name, SPARs, which stands for the Coast Guard motto in Latin and English; Semper Paratus Always Ready. The SPARs worked mainly in administrative and clerical positions ashore, freeing the men to go to sea. By the close of the war SPARS were serving in many non-traditional jobs for women such as mechanics, parachute riggers and radio operators.

Another memorable event was the successful integration of blacks. The Coast Guard was the first branch of the American military to integrate blacks. It occurred on board the SEA CLOUD, a 316-foot converted yacht assigned to weather patrol duty in the North Atlantic. There were 173 men on board the SEA CLOUD; ultimately it had four black officers and about fifty black petty officers and seamen.

The war radically changed the Coast Guard. It grew from 8,000 men to 231,000 men and 10,000 women. Coast Guard men and women provided a very broad range of service throughout the war and were highly praised by the other armed forces.

▼ By the close of the 19th century one could find blacks in posed shipboard photography. Almost always they were dressed in the distinctive steward's uniform.

(Top left) **Chief P. D.** ▶
**Autry was an Advanced
Instructor in the
Engineering and
Weapons Branch.**

(Right) **A Coast** ▶
**Guardsman stands by a
depth charge rack.**

▼ **Shown aboard a
Coast Guard attack
transport somewhere in
the South Pacific, Coast
Guardsman James
McDaniel is a loader in
a 20 mm gun crew
during action.**

Treasury Class Cutters

There were seven 327-foot Treasury class cutters built for the Coast Guard. They were DUANE, CAMPBELL, TANEY, SPENCER, INGHAM, BIBB and ALEXANDER HAMILTON. They are perhaps the Coast Guard's most famous class of cutters. They were first built in the mid-30s and some of them remained in service until the mid-80s.

As with almost all new pieces of Coast Guard hardware, these venerable vessels were severely criticized when they were commissioned. The first problem was the cost. They were $2.5 million a copy. Today, that wouldn't buy the electronic gear for a new 270, but back then $2.5 million was real money. It was nearly double the amount the Coast Guard had spent for any other cutter.

Another problem was the design and size of the cutters. There were many new design features and the cutters were big for the times; the next largest cutter had been 250 feet. Some people also complained that their towing capacity wasn't good enough and that their twin screws were too vulnerable to damage when in the ice.

The critics were silenced once the first 327, the CAMPBELL, hit the water. On her shakedown cruise, the CAMPBELL ran into a gale that delayed even the QUEEN MARY, then the largest ship in the world. The CAMPBELL easily crashed through 40-foot seas and 60-knot winds. These were powerful, tough vessels with a very smooth ride.

▼ The TANEY during World War II, probably in 1943.

Sinbad did his sea ►
duty on board the
CAMPBELL, but he is
seen here relaxing on
the front steps of his
favorite bar in Barnegat
Light, New Jersey.

Sinbad proudly wearing his World War II campaign ribbons on his collar, plays tourist while visiting Japan during the CAMPBELL's goodwill visit in the late 1940s.

Cutter CAMPBELL
at sea off England in
June, 1951.

Sinbad retired from active sea duty at ceremonies on board the Cutter CAMPBELL on September 21, 1948. Commander Gilbert I. Lynch reads Sinbad his retirement orders.

Sinbad is paw-printed for his service record. He spent a total of 15 years in the U. S. Coast Guard.

USCGC CAMPBELL

▲ The ALEXANDER
HAMILTON a month
before being torpedoed
by a German U-boat.

Their reputation was firmly established during World War II. The TANEY's exploits during the Japanese bombardment of Pearl Harbor were already mentioned. The rest of the cutters were in the North Atlantic on convoy duty during the first part of the war. The ALEXANDER HAMILTON was an early wartime casualty. It was sunk by a torpedo from the U-132 on Jan. 30, 1942; 26 Coast Guardsmen lost their lives. The remaining Atlantic-

based 327s avenged the loss of their sister ship. CAMPBELL sank the U-606, INGHAM the U-626, and the SPENCER the U-225 and the U-175.

Late in the war, the remaining 327s served as amphibious force flag ships in both the Atlantic and Pacific. TANEY served during the Okinawa campaign, where it shot down suicide aircraft.

After World War II, the Treasury class cutters continued to make Coast Guard history. On Oct. 14, 1947 the BIBB's crew performed

▲ **Coast Guard Cutter SPENCER in October, 1971. She sank two U-boats during World War II.**

▼ **CGC BIBB made one of the most dramatic rescues when she saved those on board the BERMUDA SKY QUEEN.**

one of the most dramatic rescues in Coast Guard history when they plucked 69 people from a ditched flying boat, called the BERMUDA SKY QUEEN. The TANEY served on plane guard duty during the Korean War and all six 327s served in

Vietnam. More recently, the INGHAM helped with the Cuban Boat-lift. There are countless stories about the 327s, and considering what they did over the years, that $2.5 million turned out to be money well spent.

◄ **Coast Guard Cutter INGHAM is preserved at Charleston, South Carolina.**

◄ **Another type of Coast Guard Cutter!!**

Coast Guard Auxiliary & Temporary Reserve

The pleasures and hazards of life at sea create a special bond among sailors. On the oceans, lakes and rivers people often unselfishly put their lives and property at risk to help those in distress. This seems to happen less frequently on land. This maritime bond exists among those who work on the water and those who venture out for the fun of it. This altruistic attitude is personified by the Coast Guard Auxiliary.

The Coast Guard Auxiliary, originally called the Coast Guard Reserve, was created by an act of Congress on June 23, 1939. At the time there was no military Coast Guard Reserve. Their main function was to help the Coast Guard maintain safety among the increasing number of pleasure boats.

As World War II approached the duties of these volunteers shifted along with the rest of the Coast Guard. First there was a name change. A military Coast Guard Reserve was created in February, 1941. So the volunteer

The Third Coast ▶ Guard District Auxiliary District Board holds its Board meeting on board the USCGC CAMPBELL, June 21, 1962.

◄ **Coast Guard Auxiliarists perform a courtesy marine examination.**

The Coast Guard ▶ Auxiliary is a tremendous help with our safety program. Each year, several hundred thousand people are taught boating safety.

reserve took the name Coast Guard Auxiliary. Around the same time, a Temporary Reserve also made up of volunteers, was created to help the Coast Guard with its wartime duties.

Many of the Temporary Reserve volunteers were older men or those who were not qualified for military service. Many Coast Guard Auxiliarists volunteered to serve in the Temporary Reserve while others kept up their peacetime duties in the Auxiliary.

The Temporary Reserve was created in part to patrol the Atlantic and the Gulf for enemy submarines and to report radio sightings back to the Coast Guard. The idea of using civilian volunteers and their little boats to look for U-boats may seen odd, but at the time there was little else available. The Germans were sinking one or more merchant ships a day and the United States did not have the ships to stop them. The U-boats went just about anywhere they pleased without risk of being sunk. They even went up the St. Lawrence Seaway and close to New York Harbor.

The backbone of the Temporary Reserve was the Corsair Fleet, which was made up mostly of large sailboats and a few powerboats. The volunteers had their successes. Seeing these little boats sail out to search for the elusive enemy must have been reassuring to an American public shocked by early defeats. We will probably never know their impact. U-boats needed to surface at night to recharge their batteries. Undoubtably, the boats of the Corsair Fleet caused more than one German submarine to limit its battery charge and thus restricted its operating capacity.

Corsair boats had close encounters. A German submarine surfaced underneath Willard Lewis's 38-foot weekend cruiser while he was on a patrol. The planks creaked and cracked as the boat was lifted out the water. Lewis's craft had a damaged keel but he managed to limp back to port.

Another valuable service performed by Auxiliarists and Temporary Reservists was rescue operations of victims of submarine attack. Several of these sunken ships were tankers which had burst into flames. Auxiliarists approached the very edge of the fiery water in order to pick up sailors. Many merchant sailors owe their lives to these volunteers.

After the submarine threat had diminished, Auxiliarists kept up their military assistance. A number of them volunteered to serve in the Small Ships Branch, Water Transport Division, of the U.S. Army. Often referred to as "McArthur's Navy," these Auxiliarists shipped out to New Guinea and other places in the Pacific theater to operate small craft for the general. Several were killed while assisting with the war efforts.

And while this was all going on, Auxiliarists were still promoting safety among motorboat and yacht operators. Today, this is their primary mission. The cornerstones of the Auxiliary are operations, vessel examination, education and fellowship. Through their efforts on the water and in classrooms, Auxiliarists have saved countless lives and the taxpayers millions of dollars.

**Coast Guard ▶
Reservists on the
artificial breakwater
at Normandy shortly
after D-Day.**

Typical of the U.S. Coast Guard's chain of Loran stations in the Southwest Pacific is this installation, with its towering antenna poles and gleaming quonset huts. Coined from a descriptive phrase of the system, Loran means Long Range Aid to Navigation.

Aerial view of the
U. S. Coast Guard Loran
Station, Nantucket,
Massachusetts,
June 1950.

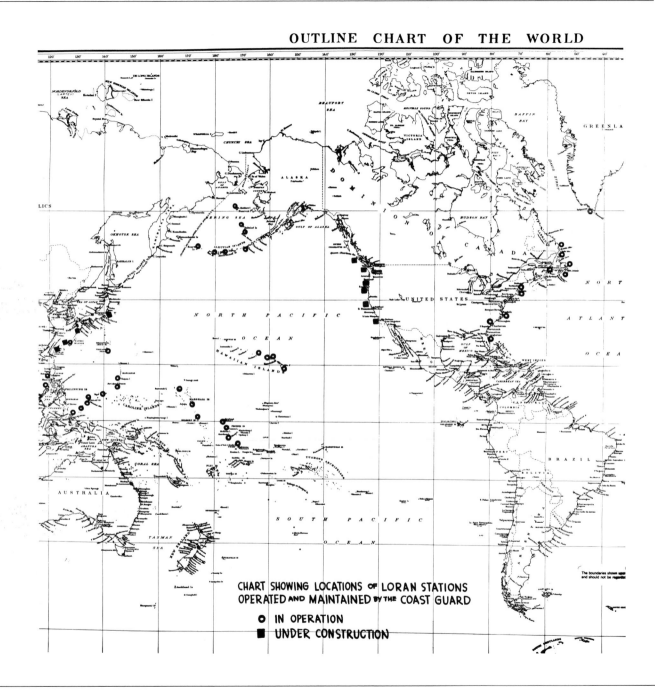

OUTLINE CHART OF THE WORLD

CHART SHOWING LOCATIONS OF LORAN STATIONS
OPERATED AND MAINTAINED BY THE COAST GUARD
○ IN OPERATION
■ UNDER CONSTRUCTION

◄ **Eager hands switch
a bag of mail from a
flying valet (Coast
Guard PBY) to Loran
Station, June 1949.**

The Mid-40s to the Mid-70s

The Coast Guard quickly returned to peacetime duties at the end of World War II, but the war and the times dramatically changed the service. The postwar Coast Guard was very different from a few years earlier.

Prior to World War I, the Coast Guard was formed in a merger of the Revenue Cutter Service and the Life-Saving Service. By the end of the World War II, the Bureau of Marine Inspection and Navigation, and the Light-house Service had merged into the Coast Guard. In addition, the World War II Loran navigation system, ocean patrols and ice operations expanded greatly. The service was now a true multimissioned organization reaching around the world.

The Bureau of Marine Inspection and Navigation put the service solidly into the merchant marine inspection and licensing business. These duties would increase in the coming years as Congress passed more anti-pollution and safety laws.

The Loran navigation system and ocean patrols became major Coast Guard duties. The Coast Guard operated 49 Loran stations in 1946. They provided to ships and planes in the Atlantic and the Pacific an accurate way to fix their positions at a reasonable cost. Both the military and the civilian aviation industry wanted this system to stay. The Service was able to convince Congress that the country's Coast Guard should be manning transmitters

◄ **View of the shielded communication room showing communication receiving equipment at a Loran Station.**

on isolated Pacific Islands and in foreign countries. A Loran modernization and expansion program was begun in 1947. This program required 57% of the service's construction budget for that year.

The 255-foot USCG ► cutter MENDOTA, bow out of the water, roughing it on ocean station "Delta" patrol, February 19, 1965.

While on weather patrol "Delta," the CGC CHINCOTEAGUE rescued the crew of the stricken German freighter HELGA BOLTEN. Life rafts, with crew, are seen here drifting toward the CHINCOTEAGUE.

Ocean Stations

The ocean patrols program was even bigger. The Coast Guard had started ocean patrols to gather weather information in 1940, but during the war, the Navy took on the major part of the task.

The Navy had 22 ocean weather stations in the Atlantic and 24 in the Pacific. After the war, the Navy announced that it was getting out of the weather patrol business. But the weather reports were still needed to assist transoceanic air commerce. So the Coast Guard expanded its ocean patrols.

Ocean patrols lasted from 1940 until 1976. The number of stations was dictated by the

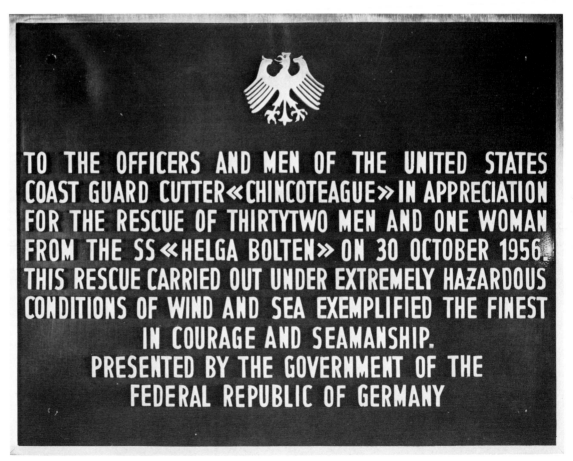

TO THE OFFICERS AND MEN OF THE UNITED STATES COAST GUARD CUTTER «CHINCOTEAGUE» IN APPRECIATION FOR THE RESCUE OF THIRTYTWO MEN AND ONE WOMAN FROM THE SS «HELGA BOLTEN» ON 30 OCTOBER 1956. THIS RESCUE CARRIED OUT UNDER EXTREMELY HAZARDOUS CONDITIONS OF WIND AND SEA EXEMPLIFIED THE FINEST IN COURAGE AND SEAMANSHIP. PRESENTED BY THE GOVERNMENT OF THE FEDERAL REPUBLIC OF GERMANY

needs of the moment and varied from one to fifteen — six were typical. Each station was located on a transoceanic air route. Cutters patrolled a 100-mile area measuring 10 miles by 10 miles. They would usually stay in the center of the square and drift in order to conserve fuel.

Ocean station duty was difficult. The patrols lasted 21 days, which did not include the time spent getting to and from the station. Coast Guardsmen would sometimes spend more than half of their time at sea; much of it in rough seas. The monotony of bouncing around in a square patch of rough water was at times broken by a rescue. There were several instances when planes in trouble intentionally landed or ditched near a Coast Guard ocean station.

The most dramatic of these rescues was the first. Gale-force winds caused the flying boat BERMUDA SKY QUEEN to use up its fuel too quickly on a trip from Ireland to Newfoundland. The plane could not make it to Newfoundland or back to Ireland. The pilot decided to land near the cutter BIBB.

The ocean landing was very difficult because of the 30-foot waves, but the pilot managed to get the fragile flying boat down in one piece. Then came the hard part — getting the passengers out of the pitching plane and onto the BIBB, which was rolling 30 to 35 degrees.

The rescue got off to a bad start. The plane taxied over to the BIBB, but because of the heavy seas, it smashed into the BIBB and damaged both the aircraft and the cutter.

An attempt to get the people off the plane with the BIBB's Monomoy pulling boat, towing a small rubber raft, failed because the rowboat could not approach the seaplane in the heavy seas.

The condition of the plane was beginning to deteriorate and darkness was approaching. The BIBB spread an oil slick to calm the waters and then three of the strongest passengers attempted to paddle a small rubber raft to the cutter. They couldn't make it to the BIBB in the heavy ocean swells, so the BIBB, drifted down to the men and picked them up with lines thrown over the side.

Just before dark, the cutter's motor surfboat towed a 15-man life raft near the aircraft and a line was passed to the plane. Then, as the gale raged on, the passengers jumped into the raft. The rescue operation took several trips but all the people were saved.

By 1976, the need for weather patrols had greatly decreased and when TANEY closed down weather station HOTEL in the Atlantic it ended an era in Coast Guard history.

Chopping ice on the CHINCOTEAGUE on Station Baker, January 1950. ►

Korea

The crossing of the 38th parallel by the North Koreans on June 25, 1950 once again plunged the United States into war. During the Korean conflict the Coast Guard remained under the Treasury Department and its wartime missions were closely related to peacetime duties.

None of the cutters was used in combat, but each played a support role along with Coast Guard aircraft. Coast Guard air detachments flew out of the Philippines, Guam, Wake, Midway, Adak and Hawaii. Their job was to protect the tens of thousands of United Nation's troops that were being airlifted across the Pacific. Additional weather station sites were also set up in the Pacific. The Coast Guard received 12 destroyer escorts from the Navy for this job.

Throughout the war, the service provided communications, meteorological, port security and ammunition off-loading services. In addition, about 50 Coast Guardsmen stationed in Korea helped establish the Korean Coast Guard, which evolved into the country's navy.

The Korean War ended when the armistice was signed on July 27, 1953. But before the signing, the Coast Guard became involved in another cold war activity on the other side of the world. The Voice of America wanted to broadcast their radio programs to more of the Balkans and Soviet-bloc nations. To accomplish this job, a 339-foot cargo vessel was turned into a floating radio station, renamed the COURIER, and anchored in the harbor of Rhodes, Greece. The vessel was manned by 90 Coast Guard officers and men. It stayed in Greek waters until a shore station was built on Rhodes 12 years later.

◄ "Iceberg Smith" was the Officer-In-Charge of the Greenland Ice Operations during World War II.

NORTHWEST PASSAGE

U.S. COAST GUARD
CUTTERS
SPAR-BRAMBLE-STORIS

◄ The Coast Guard cutter STORIS and the buoy tenders BRAMBLE and SPAR navigate through the ice attempting to find a Northwest Passage.

Ice Operations

The Coast Guard has a long history of working in very cold places. The BEAR and other cutters have worked in Arctic waters for well over 100 years. After World War II, the wind-class cutters and the MACKINAW, which was built for the Great Lakes, added significantly to the Service's ice operating ability. One of the most memorable Arctic achievements was the transit of the Northwest Passage by the cutters STORIS, BRAMBLE and SPAR.

Finding a Northwest Passage across the Arctic had been a dream of mariners for almost 400 years. The building of the Distant Early Warning radar system (DEW line) made it desirable to find alternate supply route to these remote outposts. The 230-foot icebreaking tender STORIS and the 180-foot buoy tenders SPAR and BRAMBLE set out to see if it could be done.

From almost the beginning of the trip it became apparent that the passage would not

◀ Seen here on March 15, 1971, the USCGC MAHONING leads a convoy up the icy Hudson River.

Blazing a precise ▶ trail through Beaufort Sea ice, the Coast Guard Cutter STORIS leads a flotilla of tugs and barges to Prudhoe Bay during the ice-choked 1975 Artic shipping season.

be practical for merchant ships but the three Coast Guard vessels continued their 4,500 mile journey.

To break through the heavy floes the lead ship ran its bow up onto the ice and the great weight of the ship crashed through the ice and created a channel. The vessel would then push forward and spread the ice until the cutter was stopped. The process was then repeated.

The ice floes thickened about halfway through the trip. SPAR was lifted by the ice to such an extent that it began to list to port. STORIS became lodged in the ice and

explosives failed to free the ship, so plans were made to winterize the vessels and abandon them until spring. A close inspection of the floe revealed a small crack which enabled SPAR to make a two-day, 200 yard trip to open water. After turning SPAR around, the captain was able to free the other two ships. In 64 days the cutters crossed the Arctic and became the first American ships to make the passage from the Pacific to the Atlantic Ocean, north of the North American continent. SPAR became the first ship to circumnavigate the continent in one year.

The Coast Guard's ice operations fleet was again boosted in 1965, when the Navy turned over its icebreakers to the Coast Guard. The service picked up five Navy ships and became the nation's sole icebreaking service.

Two 399-foot Polar class cutters were commissioned in the late 70s. At 13,000 tons, the Polar Star and Polar Sea are the Coast Guard's largest cutters. With their 60,000-horsepower, gas turbine engines and their massive hulls, they are capable of going wherever they are needed in the Polar regions.

Vietnam

◄ **Moving at angles during Operation Deep Freeze 1978, the powerful 399-foot Coast Guard icebreaker POLAR STAR (WAGB-10) shears away large patches of ice, cutting a wide swath through ice-paved McMurdo Sound. By riding up on the ice and dropping her weight, the POLAR STAR is capable of breaking ice up to 21 feet thick.**

Vietnam is usually remembered as a war fought in the jungles and the rice paddies. But there was another conflict as well, a sailors' war, and much of it was fought from the decks of Coast Guard cutters.

The service played a key role in securing Vietnam's 1,200-mile coastline. Coast Guards-

men destroyed enemy supply ships, supported ground units, rescued American and other friendly forces and performed many more duties. The backbone of the Coast Guard's fleet was the 82-foot patrol boat; 26 of them saw action as part of Operation Market Time. Their main job was to cut off enemy

Four 82-foot patrol ► craft of Division 11, U. S. Coast Guard Squadron One, nestle alongside their support ship, the Navy LST USS FLOYD COUNTY, on arrival at Condore Island, South Vietnam, July 29, 1965. This is the first landfall reached by the division after six days from Subic Bay.

supplies. The boats formed a picket line along the shore and covered the area with radar;

when they found a suspicious vessel they would board and search it.

This was not always easy. In July 1967, for example, a Navy aircraft pilot spotted a suspicious trawler lingering several hundred miles off the coast of Vietnam. Suspecting an enemy ship filled with guns and ammunition, he radioed Coast Guard and Navy forces off the South Vietnam coast. An ambush was set.

The patrol boat POINT ORIENT played a key role in the cat-and-mouse game that took place over the next few days. After careful study, the Coast Guard and the Navy decided the drop-off would take place on June 15th, the blackest night of the month, at Cape Batanga, an area heavily infested with Viet Cong. The Coast Guard and Navy sailors waited in ambush for the trawler.

The POINT ORIENT and a Navy PCF (Patrol Craft, Fast) lurked behind Cu Lao Re Island 12 miles off Cape Batanga, while a Navy Destroyer Escort (DE) patrolled offshore. The idea was to let the trawler safely pass the larger DE and then let the smaller Coast Guard and Navy boats intercept it nearer the drop-off point.

On schedule, the enemy steamed for the prearranged rendezvous. The DE picked up the target on radar, and quickly alerted the boats waiting behind Cu Loa Re. Then the DE let

Crew members of the ▶ USCGC POINT ORIENT and a Vietnamese Junk Force boat attached to Coast Guard Division 12, based at Danang, discuss events of 24 September 1965 as the boats lie tied together off a beach. U. S. Coast Guard 82-footer and Vietnamese Junk Force work together on coastal surveillance patrol.

◀ A crewman from the 82-foot USCGC POINT GLOVER pokes through a load of sand on board a Vietnamese junk en route to market. The inspection revealed no hidden contraband, and the men were sent on their way.

the trawler pass, closing the escape route.

As the enemy rounded the island, flares from the Coast Guard cutter lit the night, illuminating the hunters and the hunted. Realizing it had failed, the trawler dashed for the shore. With sirens screaming, the Coast Guard and Navy boats gave chase. The trawler was faster than expected. It raced ahead. The U.S. boats doggedly held on until the enemy craft reached the mouth of the Song My River, where it ran aground. A fire fight instantly broke out.

The enemy crew blazed away at the two boats with three Soviet-made heavy machine guns. But they were no match for the five .50-caliber machine guns on the Coast Guard patrol boat and the three on the PCF. The battle lasted a half hour. When it was over, the enemy trawler lay in flames where it ran aground; inside her cargo hold were enough guns and ammunition to outfit an entire regiment.

The success of interdiction operations relied heavily on the patrol boats because they could operate year round, even during the long monsoons. They were also well-armed. The 82s had five .50 caliber machine guns and an 81 mm mortar.

As in past wars, Coast Guardsmen helped the other services. Patrol boat crews worked closely with Navy SEALs and recon units, dropping them off at night and picking them up days later. They also gave emergency support to Special Forces camps, transported personnel, evacuated wounded and provided naval gun support.

About two years into Operation Market Time, naval operations were extended further offshore and expanded into the Gulf of

◀ 151. Crewmen of the Market Time U. S. Coast Guard 82-foot Cutter POINT LEAGUE (WPB-82304) battle flames on board the 100-foot steel Viet Cong trawler after the cutter forced the enemy vessel aground during a battle on June 20, 1966. The trawler attempted to infiltrate arms and supplies through Market Time patrols to the Viet Cong by way of Co Chien River.

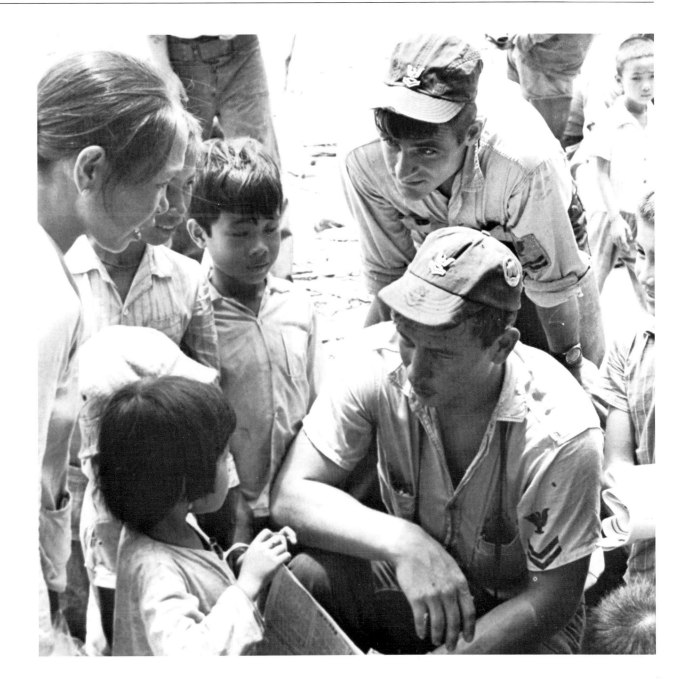

On Hom Nam Du ▶ Island, Gulf of Thailand, villagers seldom hear news about the outside world. Crew members of the USCGC POINT MAST, therefore, make a point of including Vietnamese language newspapers and magazines in their civic action packages. Electronics Technician Luther R. Winters, who speaks Vietnamese, discusses papers with the villagers as Engineman Second Class Jens H. Anderson leans over his shoulder to listen.

◄ **Officers and men on board the USCGC POINT WHITE with weapons taken from a Vietnamese junk sunk in battle with this 82-footer on March 9, 1966.**

Thailand. The Coast Guard was asked to increase its support. The service provided five high-endurance cutters. These ships ranged in size from 255 to 378 feet. They had five-inch deck guns and therefore brought with them far greater firepower than the patrol boats had. The cutters were also shallower draft than the Navy's destroyers and could bring fire from their big guns down on enemy encampments.

Shortly after their arrival they engaged the Viet Cong. The cutter RUSH, working with an Australian destroyer brought its guns to the aid of a small Special Forces camp in the village of New Song Ong Doc. The village, located in the middle of Viet Cong-held territory, was being overrun. Gunfire from the two ships halted the attack.

Like the patrol boats, the large cutters were multimission ships. They supported amphibious assaults and gave logistics support for Coast Guard patrol vessels and Navy PCFs. Medical services were given to wounded

Congressman ► Phillip Ruppe (R-Mich) receives gunnery instruction from Coast Guard Chief Boatswain's Mate Pernell J. Perry, on board the cutter POINT YOUNG while off the coast of South Viet Nam. The gentleman in the foreground is Representative Frank M. Clark (D-Penn). The visiting congressmen were touring Coast Guard facilities in Viet Nam in June 1967.

◄ **The 311-foot USCGC HALF MOON**, assigned to Area 8 Market Time, refuels vessels of the Vietnamese junk force at Hon Khoai Island, South Vietnam, September 5, 1967.

A cutter gun crew ► mans the 81 mm mortar. The mortar provided effective naval gunfire support and on several occasions saved outposts from being overrun by the Viet Cong.

WOW...The initials ► of these three high-endurance cutters spell out that expression of surprise as they nest alongside Riviera Pier at the U. S. Naval Base, Subic Bay. The three, **WINNEBAGO, OWASCO, AND WINONA,** along with a fourth unit of Squadron Three, the BIBB, were in Subic Bay for inchop, outchop, and upkeep during October 1968.

American soldiers, sailors and Marines as well as other friendly forces. These lifesaving missions were not confined to the sea leg of the Coast Guard. Coast Guard aviators were involved in saving lives during rescue missions.

Coast Guard pilots and crewmen flew Air Force HH-3E Jolly Green Giants as part of a service exchange program. Lieutenant Jack C. Rittichier served as a pilot with the Air Force 37th Aerospace Rescue and Recovery Squadron. He was an early Coast Guard combat casualty. He was killed in a mountainous region west of Danang, attempting to rescue a downed U.S. fighter pilot, when his helicopter came under hostile enemy fire and crashed in a ball of flames. Rittichier and other Coast Guardsmen flew many rescue missions over enemy-infested jungles.

Along with their combat role, Coast Guardsmen played an essential support mission. Coast Guard Port Security men were on hand as experts for safe loading and unloading of ammunition. The Explosive Loading Detachments (ELD teams) encountered their share of bizarre and deadly situations as they struggled to keep the harbors from blowing up. Fire was a constant enemy. Vietnamese families would live aboard ammunition barges, cooking with open flames, while both Vietnamese and American stevedores would smoke as they unloaded the cargoes.

Enemy attack was also a constant threat. In February 1968, at Cat Lai, a merchant ship took nine recoilless rifle hits while being unloaded. A fire started immediately. The ELD team, battling against time, rushed on board

the burning ship and doused the fire before the ship could explode.

Other Coast Guardsmen were also assigned to keeping the harbors safe. Before ships could reach the docks, they had to safely navigate into the harbors. Coast Guard buoy tenders marked the channels to help keep the traffic moving. A Loran station was set up to guide mariners and enable aviators to fix their positions.

The service also carried its humanitarian traditions to the shores of Vietnam. Coast Guardsmen carried out countless medical missions for the civilian population and helped build orphanages, schools, dispensaries, and gave of themselves in dozens of different ways.

The Coast Guard presence began to wind down as the Vietnamization program was phased in. The 26 WPBs and several large high-endurance cutters were turned over to the South Vietnamese. They became the core of their navy. An estimated 8,000 Coast Guardsmen served in Vietnam. By the time they left, Coast Guard cutters had cruised more than 5,500,000 miles, participated in nearly 6,000 naval gunfire missions and boarded nearly 250,000 junks and sampans. The service's main job was to dry up the enemy supply routes, and that they did. With Coast Guardsmen guarding the coast, an enemy junk had only a 10-percent chance of slipping through. A steel-hulled vessel had no chance at all.

◄ Buoy tending during the Vietnam conflict was a function of the Coast Guard.

157

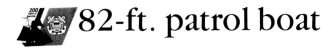

82-ft. patrol boat

The 82-foot patrol boat (WPB) in use today is a moderately high-speed patrol boat intended for use by the Coast Guard on search and rescue missions in open water under adverse weather and sea conditions.

The vessel is twin-screw, diesel-powered and capable of developing 1,600 hp. It is designed to be operated completely from the wheelhouse under normal conditions.

The WPB is powered by two Cummins model VT12-900M engines that generate 800 horsepower at cruising speed. The hull is made of 3/16 inch steel. The superstructure is made of aluminum.

The mortar machine gun used on the patrol boats in Vietnam was modified by Coast Guard Chief Warrant Officer Gunner Elmer Hicks. The weapon had several distinctive features that made it different from land mortars. It is designed for free-swing and quick changes in direction. It can be elevated to more than 70 degrees or fired in a near horizontal position.

The boat specifications are:

Length	82 ft. 10 in.
Beam	17 ft. 7 in.
Draft	4 ft. 8¾ in.
Displacement (full load)	66.1 tons
Displacement (light load)	51.8 tons
Complement	10
Provisions for	8 days
Fresh water	1271 gal.
Fuel capacity	1830 gal.
Maximum speed	23.7 knots
Cruising speed	18.5 knots
Maximum cruising distance	1,584 nautical miles
Shaft horsepower	1,600 (total)
Main engines	two Cummins Diesels #VT12-900M
Generators	two 20 KW
Armament (during peacetime)	two .50-cal. machine guns

◄ **USCGC POINT HUDSON, Division 13, on first Saigon River patrol, March 9, 1966.**

The Mid-70s to 1990

Law enforcement and environmental duties grew in importance during the mid-70s to the present. Law enforcement has probably had the greatest impact on the modern Coast Guard. This has included fisheries and drug enforcement as well as the interception of illegal migrants. In April of 1976 the United States extended its fishing sovereignty out to 200 miles. This was done mainly because large foreign fishing ships were rapidly depleting entire species. The Coast Guard was called upon to monitor the fish catches of foreign fleets and American vessels in both the North Atlantic and the Pacific.

At nearly the same time, drug smuggling began to pick up in the southern waters of the United States. The drug problem has changed the Coast Guard dramatically. Many cutters,

Fifty-six Haitians, ►
including women and small children, were crammed into a 35-foot sailboat that had left Leogane, Haiti, six days earlier. The boarding party included INS officials Harold L. Boyce (sitting) and Richard King (back to camera) and Coast Guardsmen Quartermaster Second Class George Brown and Sharon Fijalka.

◄ **Italian fishing vessel CORRADO SECONDO being inspected by COTP personnel from the USCGC TAMORA, November 1978.**

boats and aircraft have been purchased with drug interdiction in mind. The Surface Effect Ships, fast coastal interceptors, the aerostat radar units, the 110-ft. patrol boats and other pieces of hardware are geared towards stopping drugs.

The service has had some success stanching the flow of marijuana. But the increasing popularity of cocaine has created new problems; it is far easier to conceal than bulky bales of marijuana. Drug interdiction will certainly remain a major Coast Guard duty for years to come, although there may be some changes in how the service conducts the drug war as the Department of Defense becomes

more involved.

Much of the drug interdiction activities have taken place around Florida. This was also the site of a nonstop search and rescue case in 1980 — the Cuban Boatlift. In April of 1980, Castro began letting Cubans leave Mariel Harbor for the United States. Boats from the U.S. converged on Mariel and returned packed with people. It was a disorganized, dangerous rush for freedom, and when this motley collection of boats hit the turbulent waters of the Straits of Florida many of them ran into trouble.

Coast Guard units came from all over the

(Left) ► **A boarding lifeboat crew from the 378-foot Coast Guard cutter MUNRO pulls up alongside the Soviet trawler CPTM-8-56 which was caught violating fishing treaty laws off the coast of Alaska.**

(Right) ► **A gunner from POINT CHICO helps send ISLANDER, a seized drug runner, to the bottom off San Francisco.**

Atlantic Coast to help with the flood of refugees. Seventeen cutters, five boats and 16 aircraft were reassigned to Florida from other districts. In addition, entire patrol boat crews were flown in from the West Coast in order to relieve existing crews. This gave the crews a rest but not the boats. Some patrol boats put a year's worth of running time on them in only one month. Nine hundred reservists were also called to active duty to fill in for the men and women who had been assigned to Florida.

The exodus lasted about two or three months. Rescues that would have been front page news under normal circumstances barely drew any attention because they were happening all the time. When it was over, 115,000 Cubans had left their homeland for the United States.

Nineteen eighty was a busy year for the Coast Guard. Along with the Cuban Boatlift, Coast Guardsmen rescued the passengers and crew from the cruise ship PRINSENDAM. This is arguably the greatest air-sea rescue of all time. However, it has received very little attention. There are probably several reasons for this; it happened in a very isolated location, it was flawlessly executed and no one died.

The Dutch cruise ▶
ship PRINSENDAM
abandoned by 320 passengers and about 200
crew members after a
fire roared out of control, drifts in the Gulf
of Alaska.

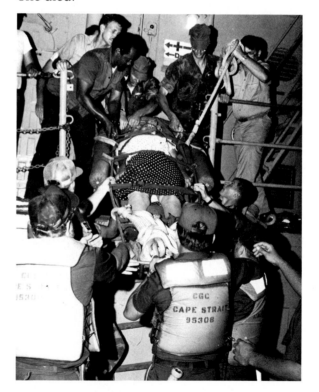

◀ (Left) **Coast Guard
Seaman Scott Albright
readies a towline on the
cutter POINT HURON
while the cutter is towing five vessels to Key
West. The POINT
HURON is stationed in
Norfolk, Virginia and
was sent to Florida to
assist with the Cuban
Boatlift, May 1980.**

◀ (Right) **A Cuban
refugee is transferred
from a Navy minesweeper to the Coast
Guard cutter CAPE
STRAIT along with 75
other refugees in the
Florida straits.**

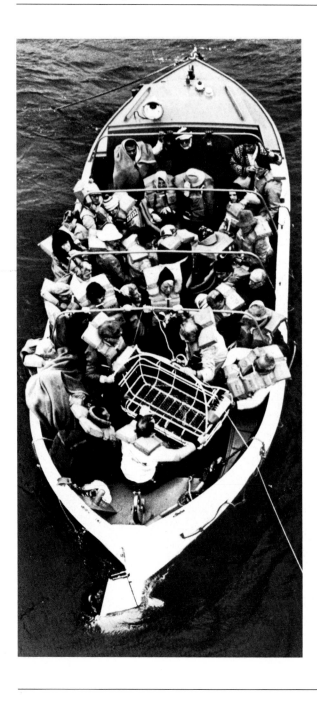

It began shortly after midnight on Oct. 4, 1980, when radiomen at Coast Guard stations in San Francisco and Kodiak, Alaska received a distress call stating that there was an engine room fire on board the the 427-foot luxury ship. The ship was in the Gulf of Alaska nearly 130 miles from the nearest airstrip. There were 519 passengers and crew on board.

The PRINSENDAM's crew battled the flames for several hours but couldn't extinguish the fire. It spread throughout the ship and finally, after the power and water pressure were lost and all fire-fighting capability was gone, the captain gave the order to abandon ship, but left a fire-fighting party on board.

A Coast Guard HC-130 out of Kodiak was the first rescue unit on scene. It arrived at about 2:30 in the morning and stayed for eight hours. The plane served as the on-scene coordinator of the rescue, directing air traffic. Next, Coast Guard long-range helicopters, HH-3Fs, began to arrive. The first ship to arrive on scene was the supertanker WILLIAMSBURG. The tanker began picking up survivors at 8:00 a.m., but it lacked the maneuverability to approach the small boats. However, the ship's two helicopter pads were of great value during the helicopter rescue.

At 9:30 a.m. Coast Guard helicopters began hoisting the survivors from the lifeboats in their baskets. Because of the distances involved, the helicopters could only make four trips before having to return for fuel. By early afternoon, the fire fighters on board the PRINSENDAM were in danger of being

◄ **Eighteen passengers from the fire-stricken cruise ship PRINSENDAM, and two Canadian paramedics lost in a drifting lifeboat were rescued by Coast Guardsmen in the Gulf of Alaska. Though the rescue is believed to be the largest involving a single ship, only one person was reported injured.**

A passenger from ▶ the PRINSENDAM walks ashore in Sitka, Alaska, wearing clothes loaned to him by the crew from the USCGC BOUTWELL.

▼ U. S. Coast Guard HH-3 helo hovers over the burning cruise ship PRINSENDAM during the rescue operations in the stormy Gulf of Alaska. The passengers and the crew were picked up from lifeboats by CG helos.

overwhelmed by the smoke and flames. The helicopters halted their rescue operation of those in the lifeboats and pulled the fire fighters off the PRINSENDAM. The cutter BOUTWELL which had recalled its crew off liberty in Juneau arrived shortly thereafter and began picking up the remaining people in the lifeboats.

The rescue had been complicated because of the great distance and the fact that several agencies were involved. Helicopters and aircraft from the U.S. Air Force and Canadian Armed Services participated in the rescue.

During rescue operations an HH-3F helicopter from Coast Guard Air Station, Cape Cod, Massachusetts, hovers over the 644-foot Liberian registered tanker SS ARGO MERCHANT after she ran aground 28 miles southeast of Nantucket Island on December 15, 1976.

The Environment

▼ Building seas whipped by high wintry winds break the SS ARGO MERCHANT in half on December 21, 1976, in spite of a six-day battle by Coast Guard units against the elements to save the tanker.

The Coast Guard's environmental duties expanded greatly in the late 60s and early 70s after a big oil well blowout in the Santa Barbara Channel followed by a series of tanker disasters. Marine Safety Offices grew, Vessel Traffic Services were set up to guide ships in busy harbors and three pollution strike teams were created. The nation's interest in environmental protection waned during the early 80s and the service scaled down its environmental safety programs. Marine Safety Offices shrunk, one of the strike teams was disbanded and the vessel traffic service program was cut back.

In the late 80s, the public's interest in the environment picked up again. Hospital waste washing up on beaches, holes in the ozone layer, acid rain and other environmental

◄ A Coast Guardsman checks the hull of the grounded Japanese cargo ship M/V SWAL-LOW in Dutch Harbor February 1989. The ship was refloated in July 1989.

Shortly after midnight on March 24, 1989, the supertanker EXXON VALDEZ grounded 25 miles south of the town of Valdez.

problems caught the public's attention. Then, the 987-foot supertanker EXXON VALDEZ ran aground in Valdez, Alaska on March 24, 1989.

Eleven of the ship's 17 tanks ripped open and more than 10 million gallons of oil spilled into the pristine waters of Prince William Sound. The public was furious. Exxon poured a massive amount of money and personnel into the cleanup operation in order to solve the problem. To date they have brought in more than 10,000 employees and spent more than $2 billion.

Hundreds of Coast Guard personnel went to Valdez. Within three hours of notification Coast Guardsmen were on the vessel sounding its tanks. By the second day Coast Guard Pacific Strike Team personnel started pumping off the remaining cargo from the EXXON VALDEZ into the EXXON BATON ROUGE. At the peak of the lightering operation, 10 pumps were transferring nearly half a million gallons of crude oil an hour. The Coast Guard supervised the removal of about three-quarters of the cargo and also directed the

The disposal of the ▶ **oil and contaminated debris was a major undertaking.**

▼ **Coast Guardsmen on the deck of the VALDEZ sounding her tanks.**

beach-cleaning efforts.

Stronger laws regulating tankers and other aspects of the oil industry are already being discussed by Congress. New laws will undoubtedly increase the Coast Guard's maritime safety duties in the near future. Taking on major new duties on short notice is not unusual for the Coast Guard. The service has spent its 200-year history bending and contorting itself to meet America's maritime needs. This latest evolution is just more

of the same.

The ability of its people to adapt to new situations has always been the Coast Guard's greatest asset. Coast Guard men and women have been told this so often that it may sound like a cliche to them, but it is the cornerstone of the Coast Guard's success. The willingness of its people to learn new tasks and then to do them well may be the only consistent thread throughout the Coast Guard's complicated history.

The 378-foot cutter ▶ RUSH, from San Francisco, served as an air traffic control center for the congested skies over Prince William Sound.

▼ USCGC IRONWOOD coordinates cleanup operations in Saw Mill Bay, Prince William Sound, Alaska in April 1989 after the VALDEZ went aground in March.

Coast Guard Vice Admiral Clyde Robbins was the Federal On-Scene Coordinator. He monitored the cleanup and filtered the many ''suggestions'' from interest groups.

Bibliography

Johnson, Robert Erwin. Guardians of the Seas: History of the United States Coast Guard 1915 to the Present, Naval Institute Press, 1987.

Kern, Florence. The United States Revenue Cutters in the Civil War (A U.S. Coast Guard Bicentennial Publication).

King, Irving H. The Coast Guard under Sail, The U.S. Revenue Cutter Service 1789-1865, Naval Institute Press, 1989.

Noble, Dennis L. Coast Guard Bicentennial Series (available from the Coast Guard historian in Washington DC).

Scheina, Robert L. Coast Guard at War (published by the U.S. Coast Guard).

Weinberg, Ellsworth A. The Volunteers: The Story of the U.S. Coast Guard Auxiliary (published by the U.S. Coast Guard Auxiliary National Board).

Willoughby, Malcolm F. The U.S. Coast Guard in World War II, Naval Institute Press, 1989.

Hecta Head Lighthouse, first lighted on March 30, 1894, and light station are among the most photographed of all the lighthouses on the West coast. Located near Florence, Oregon, its light can be seen 21 miles at sea.

This Point Arena light, Point Arena, California, was first lighted in 1908, after the first lighthouse suffered damage beyond repair in the 1906 earthquake.

(Inset) **The Graves Light-house, built in 1905, marks the northern boundary of Boston Harbor.**

Cape St. Elias Light-house is located on the southwest point of Kayak Island, Alaska. Built in 1916, this light was automated in 1974.

Guiding ships through the waters of the Florida Keys has been the job of the Sand Key light, first lighted in 1827.

Point Pinos Lighthouse, the oldest active light on the West Coast, with its original Fresnel lens, is located at the south side of the entrance to Monterey Bay. ▶

Located on a caisson at New Haven, Connecticut, Southwest Ledge Light marks a perilous underwater rock ledge.

Sentinel Island light, originally a fourth-order lens, is still active and guides ships into and through Lynn Canal to Skagway, Alaska.

Trinidad Head light is located north of Mendocina, California. The lighthouse itself is only 25 feet tall, small in comparison to others, but it sits on a hillside 196 feet above the Pacific.

▼ Hospital Point Light, located at Salem Harbor, is still active, and has served on occasion as the residence of the Commandant of the First Coast Guard District.

Point Cabrillo, near Medocino, California, originally had its light tower as part of the the fog signal building. The light is now automated and the fog signal has been replaced by a buoy with a sound device.

Wolf Trap Light, located in the Chesapeake Bay was built originally in 1870. In 1893, the light was ripped from its foundation by ice floating in the bay.

York Split Lighthouse on the Virginia coast was built in 1870.

Old Point Loma Lighthouse is a Cape Cod stone structure, and was one of the first eight lighthouses on the West coast. The lamp was first lighted in 1855, and guided ships into San Diego Harbor for 36 years until it went out of service in 1891.

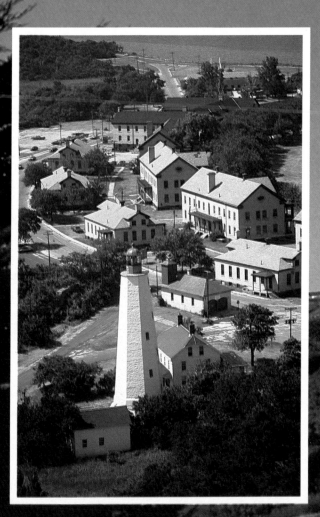

◄ Sandy Hook Lighthouse is the only surviving lighthouse of the colonial period in U. S. history. Today it is part of the Gateway National Recreation area located on the New Jersey coast.

Located northeast ► of Duluth, Minnesota, Split Rock Lighthouse was lighted by its keeper on August 10, 1910. The Coast Guard decommissioned the light in 1969, and it now serves as the focal attraction for a state park.

Four miles north of Newport, Oregon, Yaquina Head Lighthouse stands 163 feet above sea level. The lamp in its lens was first lighted on August 20, 1873.

Yerba Buena Island Light

Buffalo, New York

Alligator Reef Light is typical of the pile reef lights along the Florida coast.

Eldred Rock Lighthouse, guiding ships to Haines and Skagway, is one of the oldest surviving lighthouses in Alaska.

Maine's Boon Island Lighthouse, built in 1855, is one of the most isolated stations in Maine. In the early years, keepers had much difficulty in planting their summer gardens on this rocky site.

Located in Juneau, Alaska, at the north entrance to Cross Sound, this station received the first radio beacon in Alaska in 1926. This light is now automated, and still active.

The Boston Light is located on the site of the nation's first lighthouse. The first lamp was lighted on September 14, 1716, by the first keeper, George Worthylake.

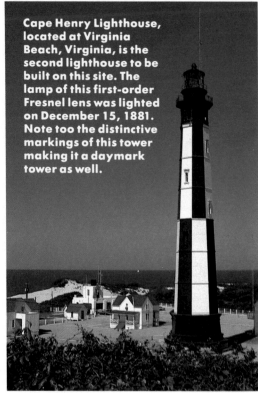

Cape Henry Lighthouse, located at Virginia Beach, Virginia, is the second lighthouse to be built on this site. The lamp of this first-order Fresnel lens was lighted on December 15, 1881. Note too the distinctive markings of this tower making it a daymark tower as well.

Charlevoix S. Pierhead Light

Cape Hatteras Light, located on the Outer Banks of North Carolina, is the tallest brick lighthouse in America, standing 193 feet tall.

This light marks the east entrance to Cleveland Harbor.

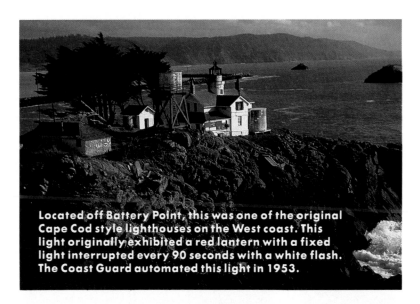

Located off Battery Point, this was one of the original Cape Cod style lighthouses on the West coast. This light originally exhibited a red lantern with a fixed light interrupted every 90 seconds with a white flash. The Coast Guard automated this light in 1953.

Drum Point Lighthouse, a screwpile light, was first lighted on August 20, 1883. The Coast Guard decommissioned this light in 1962. In 1974, the Calvert County Historical Society acquired this structure, and has moved it for restoration. It now houses the Calvert Marine Museum, Calvert County, Maryland.

Automated in 1924, the lamp of Diamond Head Lighthouse, southeast of Honolulu, is still active. Since 1939, this lighthouse has served as the home of the Commandant of the 14th Coast Guard District.

East Brother Island Lighthouse in Richmond, California, has guided traffic through the San Pablo Straits since 1874. The station is now operated as a bed and breakfast inn. The light is now automated, and is still in operation.

The 16-sided Point Reyes Lighthouse went into operation on December 1, 1870. Its original light tower still stands today.

Cape Mendocina Lighthouse, located south of Eureka, California, stands only 43 feet tall. However, because of its elevated location the light is actually 422 feet above sea level. In 1891 with the closing of the Old Point Loma Light, this lighthouse became the highest light in the Lighthouse Service.

Eastern Point Lighthouse guides ships into Gloucester Harbor, Massachusetts. Its fourth-order Fresnel lens can be seen at a distance of 13 miles.

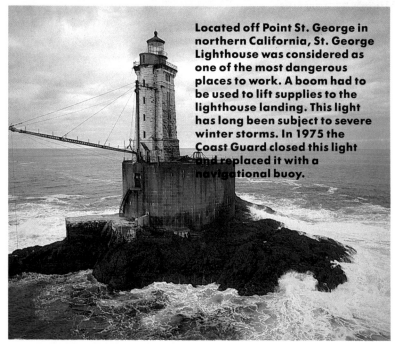

Located off Point St. George in northern California, St. George Lighthouse was considered as one of the most dangerous places to work. A boom had to be used to lift supplies to the lighthouse landing. This light has long been subject to severe winter storms. In 1975 the Coast Guard closed this light and replaced it with a navigational buoy.

P5M-1G, Marlin, was used by the Coast Guard from 1954-61. Shown here taking off from the CGAS St. Petersburg, May 21, 1955.

A Bell HH-13Q seen aboard the STORIS on Bering Sea patrol in 1961.

The HU-16E was used for air-sea rescue from 1959-1983.

A UF-2G is seen here at the USCG Air Station at Elizabeth City, North Carolina.

Sikorsky HUS-1G over Anacostia showing droppable fuel tank on her port side.

Lockheed's HC-130B was used by the Coast Guard from 1959-84.

An SC-130B Hercules seen here at the USCG Air Station, Elizabeth City, North Carolina.

The Coast Guard used eight Fairchild C-123Bs from 1960-72.

The Sikorsky Seaguard, HH-52

The Sikorsky Seaguard, HH-52, is seen here with two different color schemes.

The Sikorsky Seaguard, HH-52

190

The Sikorsky Seaguard, HH-52

Eight of the HH-19Gs were used by the Coast Guard in 1965. These were the former HO4S-3s.

This VC-Y Gulfstream was part of the USCG Detachment at National Airport, Arlington, Virginia.

The VC-4A Grumman Gulfstream II was put into service in 1965.

The Sikorsky HH-3F has been a workhorse of the Coast Guard since 1969.

The Guardian HU-25A is the new medium-range twin-engine aircraft used by the Coast Guard.

HH-65A was put into service in 1965. The Dolphin replaced all HH-52As by the end of 1988.

The Coast Guard is now using two E2Cs.

The Coast Guard's newest helicopter, HH-60J, handles many missions from drug interdiction to search and rescue.

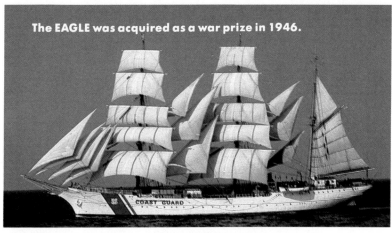

The EAGLE was acquired as a war prize in 1946.

Sister ship of the POLAR SEA, the POLAR STAR was commissioned on January 17, 1976. The sister ships are the backbone of the icebreaking fleet.

The NORTHWIND in the Arctic during 1963. The Coast Guard operated six units of this class between 1943-1989.

A 378-foot cutter, GALLATIN, one of twelve high-endurance cutters built during the 1960s and 70s. The first large U. S. warships to have gas turbine engines.

The 270-foot cutter, NORTHLAND, named for the ship that made the first naval capture during World War II.

The 110-foot cutter FARALLON named for a group of islands 50 miles to the west of San Francisco.

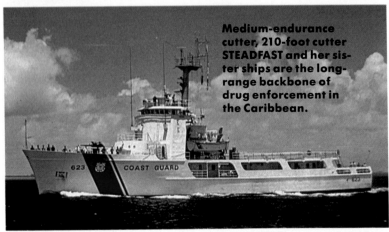

Medium-endurance cutter, 210-foot cutter STEADFAST and her sister ships are the long-range backbone of drug enforcement in the Caribbean.

Surface effect ships (called SES ships) SEA HAWK (foreground) and SHEARWATER (background) have speeds in excess of 30 knots.

Fast coastal interceptors are boats stationed in Florida waters.

POINT VERDE, an 82-foot patrol boat, is among the class of boat that was developed during the 1960s. Twenty-six of these boats served in Vietnam.

194

The 110-foot harbor tugs were in service from the mid-30s to the mid-80s.

Steel-hulled 52-foot motor lifeboat. The Coast Guard constructed four of these units.

Since the mid-60s this 44-foot self-bailing, self-righting motor lifeboat has been the backbone of the search and rescue effort afloat. One hundred six of these lifeboats were built for the Coast Guard.

A 41-foot large utility boat, built at the Coast Guard yard Curtis Bay, Maryland, between 1973-1978.

A 65-foot buoy boat, designed to service aids to navigation.

BITTERSWEET, a 180-foot buoy tender built during World War II. Thirty-nine units of this class were built, each costing less than one million dollars. Many of these tenders are still in use.

The Coast Guard has nine of these 140-foot icebreaking tugs. Despite their small size, they have about two-thirds the icebreaking capacity of the 269-foot-class icebreakers.

The river tender CIMARRON, constructed in Houston, Texas, in 1960, with its low freeboard, reveals that this class is to be used in placid river waters.

This 30-foot self-righting, self-bailing boat is designed for close-in rescue work under heavy surf conditions.

The STORIS has been in commission since 1942. She has served on many missions. Today she serves off Alaska on fishery patrol.

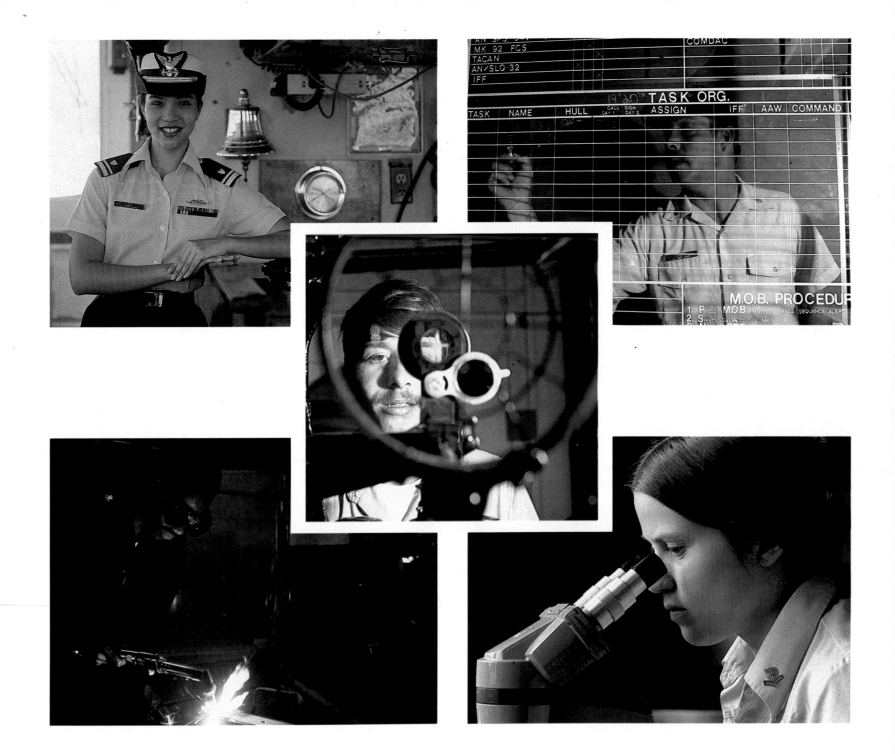

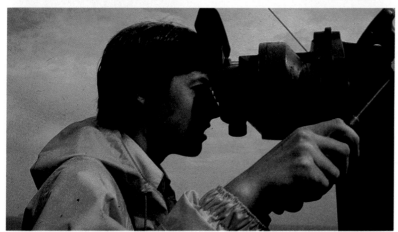

206